D1125096

Who Wants To Be
NORMAL
Anyway?!

$$E + R = O$$
$$=$$

Who Wants To Be NORMAL Anyway?!

A Teen's Guide to REAL Success and Ultimate Coolness

Kent Julian

Who Wants To Be Normal Anyway?!—A Teen's Guide to REAL Success & Ultimate Coolness
Copyright © 2011 by Kent Julian

Published by *Live It Forward LLC*
Lawrenceville, GA

CREDITS:
Cover design by Mark Holcomb
Interior design by Charles Sutherland
Edited by Andrea Reynolds

Subject Headings: Youth
                  Teenagers
                  Success
                  Personal Development

All rights reserved. No part of this publication may be reproduced, stored in a retrieval system, or transmitted in any form or any means—for example, electronic, mechanical, photocopy, recording, or any other—without the prior written permission of the publisher.

Printed in the United States of America

ISBN-13: 978-0-9777363-3-1
ISBN-10: 0-9777363-3-4

This book is available for quantity discounts for bulk purchases.

For additional information about Kent Julian, visit us on the web at **www.KentJulian.com** or email us at **booking@kentjulian.com**.

Disclaimer—
The purpose of this book is to educate and inform. The author and publisher do not guarantee particular results by following the ideas, suggestions, or strategies written about in this book. The author and publisher shall have neither liability nor responsibility to anyone with respect to any loss or damage caused, or alleged to be cause, directly or indirectly by the information contained within this book.

Dedication

This book is dedicated to my three kids—who happen to be teenagers at this moment—Chris, McKenzie, and Kelsey. I'm proud of each of you! Continue to *LIVE IT FORWARD* in the most important roles of your life.

Acknowledgements

Thank you to Mark Holcomb for your creativity and talent in designing the cover of this book. You went above and beyond, buddy!

Thank you to Charles Sutherland for your excellent interior design work. It is always a privilege to work with you.

Thank you to Andrea Reynolds, my editor. You, too, went above and beyond.

Thank you to my mom and dad for the foundation you laid in my life. Words cannot express my gratitude.

Thank you to all the teachers who invested in me during my middle school, high school, and college years. I am forever indebted.

Thank you to Jim Vaught and Dan Glaze. You two were more than educators to me, you were mentors and friends.

Thank you to the love of my life, Kathy, and my kids, Chris, McKenzie, and Kelsey, who cheered me on during this intense season of writing. I love doing life with the four of you!

Kent Julian
September 2011

Contents

REAL Success & Ultimate Coolness

Success is never an accident. It typically starts as imagination, becomes a dream, stimulates a goal, grows into a plan of action—which then inevitably meets with opportunity. Don't get stuck along the way!

—Dan Miller

I live an amazing, success-filled life!

And it all started in seventh grade!

Before we get to the it-all-started-in-seventh-grade part of the story, you should probably know a bit more about the awesomeness of my life.

An Amazing, Success-Filled Life

What makes my life so awesome is not fame or fortune, although I am fairly well known within my sphere of influence, and financially, I do pretty well. Yet the truth is, I started experiencing true success *way before* my bank account was full or anyone knew anything about Kent Julian.

Early on, I learned that *real* success can be accomplished by anyone . . . even someone as average, or below average, as me. So early on, I went after achieving real success!

The results?

First off, I am married to the most amazing woman on the face of the planet! Kathy is gorgeous on the outside, but more importantly, she's gorgeous on the inside as well. As I like to say, "I definitely out punted my coverage" when Kathy accepted my hand in marriage. We love each other deeply and have worked hard to develop an awesome marriage.

Together, we have three children that we love dearly. While our family isn't perfect (what family is?), we are very close and cherish doing life together. Both quality and quantity time are the norm for us, so much so that many of my kids' friends hang out at our house. Kathy and I have heard several say that our family is not "normal" because we have tons of fun together, we have each other's backs, we talk openly and honestly about life, and we truly love each other. If this kind of family life is not "normal," then we're cool with not doing "normal."

Professionally, I've experienced significant success in multiple careers. My first career path involved leading several youth programs that worked with middle school and high school teenagers. I did well in this career path, so well, in fact, that by my early 30s I was the executive director of a national youth organization that worked with approximately 2,000 youth groups all across the nation.

> The secret of success in life is for a man to be ready for his opportunity when it comes.
>
> —Benjamin Disraeli

My second career path, the one I am currently traveling, actually involves several "jobs." I started Live It Forward LLC (www.liveitforward.com), a company that offers both life and career coaching, as well as executive coaching. Additionally, I am a keynote speaker and trainer for students and educators (www.KentJulian.com), which allows me to speak to thousands of people across America every year.

On a personal level, I have reached or am in the process of reaching many of the goals I have set for myself, including athletic, academic, financial, and personal development goals. I am actively involved in serving my community. I am even the head coach of a swim team with approximately 160 swimmers ages four to eighteen years old that competes in one of the largest swim leagues in the country.

Again, I live an amazing, success-filled life!

But . . .

The beginning of my story was anything but amazing.

My Story

In elementary school, I was a loser and I knew it. It's not as though I was depressed or unhappy; I was one of those nice kids that got along with everyone. However, I did struggle. Academically, I had a significant speech impediment and could not pronounce the sounds associated with the letters "f, g, j, k, l, r, v, s, z, ch, sh, th, and related consonant blends." Additionally, by the time I reached third grade, my teacher had a private conference with my parents and asked how I had passed the previous grades without being able to read. Simply put, I wasn't the sharpest tack in the box.

Physically, I wasn't much to look at either. I was short, chubby, and wore Tough Skin Jeans. (You probably have no idea what Tough Skin Jeans are, so just think of the dorkiest pair of pants a kid could wear, and that's what I had plastered on my chunky little body.)

> Confidence is contagious
> So is lack of confidence.
> —Vince Lombardi

But what was most difficult for me was my lack of athletic ability. I loved sports, but my arms and legs never supported that passion. Let's just say when it came time to choose teams for kick ball, I prayed not to be picked last. That way, at least I knew I wasn't the biggest loser on the playground.

Bottom line . . . the word "confident" was not in my vocab.

When I hit middle school I grew, so fast, in fact, that by the beginning of eighth grade I was almost as tall as I am now. Along with this growth spurt came some athletic ability, not a ton, but enough that I decided to try out for the middle school basketball team in seventh grade. Jim Vaught, the middle school coach, decided to keep 15 players that year. When he met with me, he told me I was the last person to make the team. The conversation was not an aren't-you-lucky speech, but more of an I-believe-in-you chat. He told me I probably wouldn't see a ton of playing time, but if I worked hard, next year could be a different story. To be honest, I wasn't really listening; I was just thrilled to make the team. In my mind I would never be a real athlete, so just being associated with jocks was a step up from my loser status. I still wasn't confident, but at least now, I could fake like I was.

During the season, I made a major personal mistake; something that to this day I am still ashamed of doing. The details aren't necessary; just know, it was *major!* When Mr. Vaught called me into his office to confront me about my alleged transgression, I had no idea I had been caught. When he dropped the bomb, I was devastated. The mistake was bad enough, but at that moment I realized my parents, my teachers, and a basketball coach who believed in me were all disappointed. All the confidence that was budding within me was cut short.

Or was it?

Mr. Vaught helped turn a potentially devastating situation into a positive watershed moment in my life. He was firm. He was even disappointed. Yet he still believed in me. I could sense it. I saw it in his eyes and heard it in his words. Even in the midst of saying some very hard things to me, I knew he believed I was a special kid with a special future. He clearly communicated that my tomorrow did not need to be created from my yesterday; that my future was still in the future. He challenged me to own up to my mistake, seek forgiveness, learn from it, and move on.

At the end of the season, Mr. Vaught pulled me aside for another chat. The incident had happened only a few weeks earlier, so I had been avoiding Coach. I'd see him in math class and at basketball practice, but always kept my distance. So at first, when he wanted to talk I was afraid he was going to rehash my mistake. Instead, all he said was, "Kent, I think you could get significant playing time next year if you work hard this summer. I really do!" When next year rolled around, not only was I starting, I led the team in scoring.

At the awards ceremony, Mr. Vaught stood in front of a packed gym and said something along these lines: "I want to recognize Kent Julian. Last year he was the last person picked for the team. This summer he dedicated himself to practicing four to five hours a day. Because of his efforts, he was our most improved player, our leading scorer, and our most valuable player."

Nice words, huh? Almost thirty years later, I have a hard time writing them without getting choked up. But honestly, Jim Vaught left out one, very important detail. I accomplished those things because he believed in me. If he had handled my watershed moment any differently, those words would have never been uttered, at least not about me. My relationship with Mr. Vaught—a teacher and coach who saw me at my very worst, yet chose to believe in my absolute best—was what inspired me. Because he believed in me, I started to believe. And it didn't just affect my basketball skills, confidence spilled over into other areas of my life as well.

What You Didn't Know About Me

Before reading my seventh grade story, here's what you knew about me:

- I am happily married and head-over-heels in love with my wife.
- I passionately love my family.
- I led several large youth organizations, including a national one.
- I am a successful entrepreneur.
- I speak all over the country to thousands of students and educators every year.

As you read my seventh grade story, you discovered:

- I had a significant speech impediment as a child.
- By the time I reached third grade, I still could not read.
- I had little, if any, confidence.

But what you still don't know about me is:

- In seventh grade I was an "at-risk" kid, struggling academically, hanging out with the wrong crowd, and making some very poor choices.
- Even though I worked hard in high school and improved my grades, my academic challenges continued all the way into college. In fact, when I graduated high school, my SAT scores were so low that I had to take Developmental Studies after graduation just to get accepted into college on probation.

You also didn't know that I ended up:

- Graduating from college with Cum Laude (high) honors.
- Earning a Masters of Arts degree with Summa Cum Laude (highest) honors.

Your Story

My story started out pretty rough. I wasn't a smart or gifted kid. In fact, I wasn't even average; I was below average.

> *You can have life or you can make life. In the first case life happens to you. In the second, you happen to life.*
> —Michael McClure

While I had challenges, the start to my story is much less challenging than the start to other people's story. Sure, I struggled with confidence. I had a significant speech impediment and academic problems. There were even times when I traveled the at-risk path. But I know others whose stories include challenges much greater than mine—serious illness, abuse, neglect, even self-destructive behavior.

But my story is my story.

And guess what?

Your story is your story.

So, just like me, you have to live your story.

Your start might have been easier than mine. Or, it might have been ten times more difficult. That's not the point. The point is . . . we each have a story, and we each have to live out *our own* story.

In fact, there are three things that are true about each of our stories:

- Our story is *our* story, nobody else's.
- We cannot change what has been written so far in our story—that ink has already dried.
- We are 100 percent responsible for what will be written in our story—that ink is still in our pens.

THAT DAY . . . Everything Changed!

Up until seventh grade, my story was anything but awesome.

Then . . .

In seventh grade, on one particular day, everything started to change!

Things did not change all at once; in fact, some changes did not occur for months. Others took years. Even today, I am striving to make changes in my life. So saying "everything started to change" in seventh grade does not mean that I no longer made mistakes, that I suddenly became perfect, or that everything became easy for me. Not at all!

However, what started to change was my *mindset*.

You see, up until seventh grade I was a loser and knew it. Or perhaps a better way to say this is, "I *thought* I was a loser and knew it." In my mind, I wasn't smart enough, good looking enough, or talented enough to ever be successful, so I was willing to settle for being "below average." Or maybe . . . just maybe . . . if I pushed myself . . . I could actually reach "average." (Yeah, I know—not exactly inspiring!)

But again, in seventh grade, my *thinking* started to change. In the midst of a major mistake, instead of moving backwards, I started pushing forward. Instead of blaming the kid

> *Success is the progressive realization of worthwhile, predetermined, personal goals.*
>
> —Paul J. Meyers

who turned me in or getting ticked off at the teacher who dished out my punishment, I decide to learn what I could from my misstep. I decided not to follow the "normal" pattern and make excuses; instead, I took ownership. And that's when everything started changing! That is the moment I took my first step towards an amazing, success-filled life.

REAL Success and Ultimate Coolness

Most people's understanding of success is pretty screwed up. It usually revolves around fame and fortune, and while each of these can be a result associated with success, neither is actually a definition of success.

Real success is best defined through embracing a *Live It Forward* life.

So what exactly is a *Live It Forward* life? Allow me to take you to a special place of imagination. Since you're reading this, I cannot ask you to close your eyes, but I will ask that you read S-L-O-W-L-Y . . . stopping every once in a while to allow the scene I am about to describe to soak in and become vivid in your mind. Feel it. Hear it. Touch it. See it.

Okay, here goes . . .

You enter a large room unnoticed. You are not sure why you are there; you just know you are supposed to be present.

The first thing that strikes you is the room is overflowing with people. It's packed. Wall-to-wall.

You also notice it is a formal occasion, and you begin to sense a mixture of gratitude and joy along with sadness and sorrow. It feels sort of strange—celebratory, yet heartrending.

There are seats in the room, and they are arranged in such a way that you realize there is going to be a presentation. Additionally, you notice a large, strange box, along with a microphone, at the front.

You continue to be amazed with the "feel" of this place. Smiles and hugs mixed with tears. It is the people present who make the room feel so warm, comforting, and thankful; yet, again...sad.

The formal ceremony starts and you still go unnoticed, sitting in the shadows in the back of the room. One by one people stand and speak about a person—as if each is introducing this individual to those in attendance . . . yet . . . not. Each presenter tells stories that reveal this person as being someone of outstanding character who has a passion for life and has impacted others. They describe an individual who seems heroic and, at times, larger than life . . . yet very much human and authentic.

What is even more amazing is that the people speaking are not star-struck fans who view this person from a distance. They represent those closest to this person. The first speaker is a son. The second, a daughter. Then a neighbor shares, along with a co-worker, followed by a community leader. Finally, the spouse speaks. Each person shares stories and insights from their perspective, and while each perspective is different, each ends up communicating the same wonderful sort of things about this person.

The love in the room is so rich you can feel it. The respect and appreciation so thick you can reach out and touch it. Again, there is sadness, but the sadness is bested by admiration and gratitude.

As the ceremony ends, most people linger, continuing to share stories with one another. Still unnoticed, you wander to the front of the room to examine the oddly shaped box. As you approach, you stop and stare.

It's a coffin!

Do you dare look inside?

You move closer.

Finally, you peer over the side.

To your utter amazement, you know this person.

In fact, you know this person very well.

The person is YOU!

Nothing defines a *Live It Forward* life better than this story. Simply stated, living it forward means to determine ahead of time what you want said about your life at your funeral, and then to go about living in such a way as to guarantee those things will be said. It's writing your life's script ahead of time, and then daily living that script into reality!

I know, thinking about your funeral is sort of morbid. What's more, your funeral is likely a long, long way away. In fact, you probably do not have your career path mapped out yet, I doubt you are married, and having kids is something

NOTE: I was originally introduced to the "attend your own funeral" concept through Stephen Covey's book *The Seven Habits of Highly Effective People*. This book is one of the most impactful books I have ever read. If you want to live it forward in the most important roles of your life, READ IT!

that I am guessing is a long way off for you. So why in the world would you think about what any of these people are going to say at your funeral?

Because every really successful person you will ever meet thinks this way. So, if you want to join their ranks, it makes sense to develop the same mindset!

Seriously, if you really want to experience a truly successful life—a life of significance that positively impacts others in an amazing way—then it's time to start thinking about more than just what you've got going for the weekend. What positive qualities do you want to be known for? What contributions do you hope to achieve? And how will you "live it forward" so that these character qualities and accomplishments become a reality of your life?

Who Wants to be Normal, Anyway?!

On that particular day in seventh grade, I stopped being "normal." I still looked pretty average, but on that day I took my first steps towards a *Live It Forward* life and everything started to change for me!

This book is a guide to help you stop being "normal." I mean, come on, if you think about it, do you really want to be "normal?" "Normal "is defined as *conforming to a standard; usual, typical, or expected.* Is that what you want out of life? Conformity? Usual? Typical? Expected?

Not me!

I hope not you, either.

The Top 3 Percent

Specifically, this book is designed to help you move from the top 50 percent, to the top 10 percent, to the top 3 percent of people. And I don't mean the top 3 percent in a "stuck up, nose-in-the-air, cocky, I'm-better-than-you-and-I-make-more-money-than-you" sort of way. Being in the top 3 percent does not necessarily mean fame and fortune; it means you are one of the few who makes a significant contribution with your life while flat out loving what you do!

We will start in Section One by looking at ten habits that will help you move into the top 50 percent bracket. I call these realities the *LIVE Smart* stuff you have to do if you want to achieve at least an average life.

In Section Two, we will look at ten strategies that will help you leapfrog your way into the top 10 percent category. These are strategies that will cause you to realize that *It's Your Life, Own IT!*

Finally, in Section Three, we will learn about ten more principles that can put you in the same 3 percent category of the most truly successful people on the face of this planet. Every one of these people realizes that *FORWARD is the Direction of Success!*

Before We Begin

Before we begin, here are a few things that will help you get the most out of our little adventure together.

First, while this is an easy read, it's not a shallow read. This means I want you to stop and chew on what you read (please don't literally "chew" on the pages unless you're a gerbil). As you do, let the ideas steer you towards action.

Second, I didn't write this book because I have it all together. If you think speakers and authors have it all together, you have my permission to slap yourself in the face right now because you're in La-La Land. I'm not perfect, not even close. So while I talk a lot about success in this book, keep in mind that I'm not writing as someone who has arrived. Like you, I'm a fellow traveler in life's journey. What makes my perspective on success different is I'm a bit older than you, so I'm further down the road. And even more importantly, I've been a life-long student of the habits and character traits that make people truly successful. I've interviewed a bunch of successful people and read a truckload of books about success. I've even tried to put most of what I've learned into practice. So that's why I write—to share what I've learned so that it might help you along your success journey.

Third, some chapters will connect with you and others probably won't. This book shares 30 ideas that have worked for me, but I'd be nuts to think they'd all connect with you. So read and apply whatever strikes your fancy, then ignore the rest (feed those pages to the gerbil I just mentioned). Believe me, you won't hurt my feelings.

BIG is Little and Little is BIG

Finally, let me share one of my favorite sayings with you: *BIG is little and little is BIG.* Whenever I speak to student audiences, I ask if they want to:

- Find a career that they love so much that they never feel like they are going to work?
- Develop meaningful friendships that will last the rest of their lives?
- Experience an incredible marriage and a happy family life?
- Positively contribute to their community?
- Make a ton of money providing a valuable service or product?
- Impact the world in significant ways?

After each question, audience members throw their hands up and shout back: "ABSOLUTELY!" And that's when I tell the audience that *BIG is little and little is BIG.*

You see, everyone wants to experience the big positives in life—a happy marriage, meaningful friendships, a career they love, and opportunities to make a significant contribution to the world. But the secret to experiencing the big things in life is getting the little things right day in and day out. It is realizing that every day we make little decisions that will either lead us closer to or further away from the big successes we all want.

This book focus on those little things which, if done daily, will help you get the big things you want out of life.

BIG is little and little is BIG!

LIVE Smart

Being stupid is its own reward.

—Anonymous

It's amazing how many people live dumb!

Notice, I did NOT say: "It's amazing how many people *are* dumb." What I said was: "It's amazing how many people *live* dumb." There is a big difference!

You don't have to be Captain Obvious to realize there are a lot of humans walking around this planet who act in a less-than-intelligent manner and do some outright stupid stuff. Then they wonder why life doesn't work out for them. Go figure.

Since you are reading this book, I'm assuming you want to avoid major missteps that will put you in the bottom 50 percent bracket. If so, the habits in this section are really basic, but still really powerful. Apply them, and you are guaranteed to live at least an "average" life.

I call these *habits to survive.*

CHAPTER 1

SIMON SAYS WHAT?

*Life is like a Simon Says game. It's designed
to get you out!*

—Kent Julian

In a lot of my presentations, I state: "Life is like a Simon Says game. It's designed to get you out."

I know, I know . . . I'm supposed to be an upbeat, positive, motivational speaker.

Okay, so let me try this again.

And tell you what, I'll be more positive.

Here goes!

"I'm POSITIVE . . . life is like a Simon Says game. It's designed to get you out!"

The Cold, Hard Facts

Life's tough, especially if you strive for success. As Jim Rohn says, "All good things in life are upstream, but the natural flow of life has a downward, negative pull."

This truth isn't a party. And if you're like me, you wish life wasn't this way. But it is. Anyone telling you different is selling you a load of something.

What this means is that although we all want the good stuff in life—healthy relationships, a great career, financial freedom, and more—most people, just as in a Simon Says game, end up getting out. Again, I hate to be the bearer of bad news, but this is just . . . well . . . normal.

Pay Attention!

How can we outsmart the Simon Says game of life and avoid "getting out?" Simple. Pay attention! That's right, pay attention.

The sad truth is "normal" people coast through life never paying attention to what's going on around them. They are so distracted by all the noise and commotion that they miss opportunities staring them right in the face or unknowingly skip into disasters that are standing right in front of them. If they would just pay a little more attention, they would see people who:

- Are royally screwing up and what consequences those people are having to endure,
- Are accomplishing significant stuff and learn how these people did it and what positive benefits they are reaping,
- Are developing real friendships and what they are doing that "normal" people don't do,
- Are authentically happy and why they are happy.

Stop being "normal" like everyone else. Stop coasting! Open your eyes and ears and start paying attention to life around you. Within a nanosecond you'll recognize habits and actions you can take to win the Simon Says game of life.

You can tell when you are on the road to success. It's uphill all the way.

—Paul Harvey

STOP Being "Normal"
Action Steps

List at least three people who seem to be winning at the Simon Says game of life. Watch them this week to see how they avoid "getting out" (or, if you're gutsy enough, interview them). See if you can figure out what they are doing that is different than what "normal" people do.

1. _____

_____

_____

_____

2. _____

_____

_____

_____

3. _____

_____

_____

_____

_____

CHAPTER 2

CHECK YOUR INSTRUMENTS

*Watch the little things; a small leak
will sink a great ship.*

—Benjamin Franklin

I have a friend who was an Air Force pilot. He explained to me that if a pilot climbs into the cockpit and does everything absolutely right *except* he calculates his landing position wrong by just one tiny degree, here's what happens:

- After 100 miles, the plane will be off course by 1.6 miles,
- After 1,000 miles, the plane will be off course by 16 miles,
- After 10,000 miles, the plane will be off course by 160 miles.

Wow, if you're flying to Alaska and you're off by one degree, you can end up in Russia instead of Anchorage.

Lead Your Life from Quiet

We make thousands of tiny decisions every day. Some good; some bad. Some move us closer to success; some lead us further away. Yet, one of the differences between living smart and living dumb is that successful people take time to examine their decisions because they know that even a small mistake can turn into a major blooper over time.

It's not that successful people slam on the brakes and pull out a microscope to examine every little decision. *Hmmmm . . . let's list out all the pros and cons of sinking my teeth into today's mystery meat selection in the cafeteria. Then, I'll use the Arrhenius equations to calculate the chemical kinetics . . .* (you get my point). Successful people, just like "normal" people, take time to stop and think about the big decisions they face. However, what separates them from "normal" people is that successful people also take time to think through the small decisions; they just don't examine every tiny decision in the moment.

So when do they do it? Great question! (I knew you were smart.) The answer is they think about all the small decisions and how those decisions are impacting their lives when they lead their lives from quiet.

Later on in this book, I'll explain in detail a success habit I call *Lead Your Life from Quiet*; but for now, here's a teaser. Successful people carve out time, at least weekly—but most do it every day—to slow down, get quiet, and review life. Some journal. Others pray. Some just sit and think. Different people do different things, but the point is, successful people have a regular habit of slowing down and thinking about what's going on in their lives.

Want to live smart? Then you might want to slow down and spend some time leading your life from quiet.

It is important from time to time to slow down, to go away by yourself, and simply be.

—Eileen Caddy

STOP Being "Normal"
Action Steps

"Normal" people don't slow down enough to figure out if their lives are off by one degree, ten degrees, or 90 degrees. But you're not "normal." What steps will you take this week to slow down and check to see if you're off by a few degrees?

_____

_____

_____

_____

_____

_____

_____

_____

_____

_____

_____

_____

_____

_____

CHAPTER 3

"Chuck Norris" Your Potty Mouth

Profanity is the weapon of the witless.

—Anonymous

One of my daughters got off the school bus one day and said, "Man, our bus is worse than an R-rated movie! Fewer than half the kids can't complete a sentence without dropping the f-bomb!"

You might think I'm a bit of a geezer on this one, but how ridiculous is it to drop cuss words in as adjectives or adverbs? Someone's peanut size brain can't squeeze out a useful descriptive word, so he throws in several "bleeps" to make his point. Why not just stand up with a megaphone and shout, "I'm an idiot!"

I'm telling you right now, people who have rich relationships, great jobs, and meaningful lives have long ago "Chuck Norris-ed" their potty mouths. Why? Because they know colorful language doesn't make them colorful . . . it makes them stupid (or at least appear that way). Cussers sound negative, unintelligent, undependable, and out of control. Seriously, foul language won't *ever* make you look good. It automatically knocks you down a few notches in the eyes of anyone with any amount of class.

Five "Chuck Norris" Moves

If you want to stop cussing, here are five "Chuck Norris" moves that will help you get control of your potty mouth.

Move #1—Know your *why*. When breaking a bad habit, you need to know your *why*. Why do you want to stop cussing? Come up with your own list, but at the top, please write something like: "This is dumb. If I keep cussing, I'll end up in the bottom 50 percent bracket. If I ever want to be in the ballpark of real success, I better live smart and break this habit NOW before it is impossible to break."

Move #2—Pay attention. We already mentioned how important it is to pay attention to what's going on around us, so this isn't a new concept. If you pay attention to what you say and what your friends say, you'll quickly notice every time someone swears. Simple awareness is a great step towards stopping.

Move #3—Grow your vocabulary. Using cusswords as descriptors is a sign of lazy speech. So next time you're tempted to pull the pin on a 4-letter grenade, replace it with a real adverb or adjective that better conveys your idea or emotion. In fact, make a game of it with your friends—see who can come up with the best word. You could even use a dictionary or thesaurus on your smart phone. You'll probably bust a gut laughing at some of the words you come up with as you grow your vocabulary at the same time.

Move #4—Get support. Speaking of your friends, how about asking a few non-swearers for help. Level with them about your habit and ask them to help you break it. To be honest, they're probably tired of listening to all the refuse spewing from your lips, so they'll be excited to help out. They know you are a better person than this, and they'll be glad you finally figure out something needed to change.

Move #5—Punish and reward yourself. Every time you cuss, make it hurt! Don't smack yourself, but do something that will cause pain. I didn't have to do this with cussing, but to break some bad grammatical habits I enlisted a good friend to charge me a nickel every time I messed up. I ended up owing her more than $45—no lie! But I finally broke the habit. And what's really cool . . . once broken, she took me out for dinner to celebrate.

Hang Tight

Remember, big is little and little is big. That means stopping this big, bad habit requires a bunch of daily, baby steps. You won't stop dropping "blankety-blank bombs" overnight; but eventually, those baby steps will lead to the big success of being cuss-free!

My Favorite Chuck Norris Facts:

When Chuck Norris jumps in the water, he doesn't get wet. The water gets Chuck Norris-ed.

Ghosts sit around the campfire and tell Chuck Norris stories.

Chuck Norris doesn't call the wrong number, you answer the wrong phone.

Chuck Norris makes onions cry.

Chuck Norris can eat soup with chopsticks.

Chuck Norris and Superman once fought each other on a bet. The loser had to start wearing his underwear on the outside of his pants.

Darth Vader dresses up as Chuck Norris for Halloween.

STOP Being "Normal"
Action Steps

Do you need to "Chuck Norris" your potty mouth? Pick at least three of the five steps listed in this chapter and describe how and when you plan to implement them.

Step: _____

How will you apply it? _____

_____

By when? _____

_____

Step: _____

How will you apply it? _____

_____

By when? _____

_____

Step: _____

How will you apply it? _____

_____

By when? _____

_____

CHAPTER 4

PEER FEAR

*Peer pressure can shake your confidence and is much
greater than most adults realize.*

—Joanna, 16 years old

Do you like coming attractions? You know, movie previews? I love them!
But a few years ago, a particular preview freaked me out. It had eerie sights
and sounds along with the intense catch phrase: *Be Afraid . . . Be Very
Afraid.* Let's just say I almost had an accident!

Be Afraid . . . Be Very Afraid

What makes you *afraid . . . very afraid?* Since no two people are alike,
what frightens one person can energize another. However, there is one
thing that makes practically everyone's teeth chatter. The fear of REJEC-
TION!

Fear Factor

The anxiety of rejection—of not being accepted—is at the root of what
experts call *peer pressure*. It's the stress associated with the desire to "fit in"
that we all feel. For many people, teens and adults alike, this stress mo-
tivates everything . . . dress, speech, behavior . . . everything! In fact, it's
a lot like the television show *Fear Factor* from a few years ago. Like most
game shows, contestants competed for prizes. But what made *Fear Factor*
different were the challenges contestants faced—each one revolved around
fear. Jumping from one motorboat to another at speeds of 40 mph. Navi-
gating an obstacle course on the ledge of a ten-story building. Swimming

25

in a tank of dead, rotting squids or eating cow brains. Each experience was designed to see exactly how far someone would go to overcome fear.

A lot of teens go to unimaginable lengths to avoid rejection; some that could even put *Fear Factor* contestants to shame. As Drew, an eighth grader in Omaha once told me, "What I think my friends want controls me. I talk, act, and even dress like them to fit in."

Did you notice what controls Drew? It's not necessarily the pressure put on him by friends, it's the pressure *he places on himself.* He "thinks" his friends want certain things, so his thoughts, whether legit or not, control him.

This is why I think a better phrase for peer pressure is *peer fear.* Much of the anxiety we feel comes from the inward fear of being rejected, not from outward pressure by peers. The pressure from friends, while at times real, can just as often be imaginary.

Taming Peer Fear

How can we tame peer fear? Try these ideas . . .

Pay attention to timing. Peer fear tends to be a bigger deal in middle school and the first couple of years of high school than later on in high school and college. If you are in the first half of your teen years, just knowing this fact helps you realize it won't always feel this intense.

Look for signs. Signs that made me think Drew was struggling with peer fear were his massive desire to impress friends, sudden changes in vocab, dramatic fashion modifications, and moodiness. If you see similar signs in your life or a friend's life, peer fear might be a bigger deal than you think.

Know what peer fear is and what it is not. There's nothing wrong with fitting in. We all want to connect with a group of friends. It's the codependent thing that isn't healthy. Look at your life . . . do you have a healthy balance between connecting with friends and your own personal confidence? If so, you're probably doing just fine. However, if you can't "live without your friends," or if they influence you to do things you don't want to do (or worse, you know shouldn't do), watch out!

Choose NOW to walk away. When a group of friends starts screwing around, it's tough to be the only one who says "no." But if you are living smart, then most of the time it's going be clear what's right and what's wrong. And while it still may be tough to stand up for what's right, if you make a commitment to stand firm in your convictions and walk away *before* you are in the heat of the moment, it's going to be easier to follow through.

Tap into positive peer pressure. Did you know peer pressure doesn't have to be a bad thing? If you live smart and choose friends wisely, you won't feel as much pressure to lie, cheat, gossip, cut class, smoke, do drugs, or whatever. You'll actually face a different type of pressure—positive peer pressure. You'll feel the pressure to study and achieve your goals. That's good pressure!

Tap into positive, adult role models. Want to pack more force behind the positive peer pressure punch? Then seek out positive role models such as parents, teachers, coaches, school organization advisers, or leaders in the community. We'll talk more about adult mentors in Section Two, but just know that mentors will not only help you deal with peer fear, they can also give insights into life that friends your age simply don't have yet.

Be a friend. A great way to overcome peer fear is to reach out and help others. Is there a new girl in class? Welcome her and show her around. Is there a guy who is having a hard time fitting in? Man up and help a brother out! Your personal struggle with peer fear will shrink into a wimpy shadow if you step out of your comfort zone and help someone else.

Respect peer fear. Finally, always remember that peer fear is probably the single biggest cause of someone straying off the "live smart" path. That means you need to have a healthy respect for its power. Don't let it paralyze you, but don't blow it off either. And by all means, if you see signs of peer fear in your life, tap into your positive peer pressure friends and the adult role models. They'll help you get back on track.

There's one advantage to being 102. There's no peer pressure.

—Dennis Wolfberg

STOP Being "Normal"
Action Steps

How are you doing with peer fear? Journal your thoughts here:

_____

_____

_____

_____

_____

_____

_____

_____

_____

_____

_____

_____

_____

_____

_____

CHAPTER 5

RIPPING OFF YOUR UPSIDE-DOWN GLASSES

Reading is to the mind what exercise is to the body.

—Joseph Addison

I found this story in a file and have no idea where it came from. But after you read it, you'll see why I'm sharing it with you.

A number of years ago, a scientist performed an interesting experiment. He strapped a strange set of eyeglasses, which looked like binoculars, on several people. The participants willingly wore these glasses every hour they were awake. Inside the lenses, several mirrors enabled the wearers to see everything upside down. At first they tripped over furniture and were unable even to walk. They could barely sit upright without falling over.

However, after a few weeks of wearing the glasses, their eyes adjusted and they were able to see everything right-side up again. They could not only sit up and walk without problem, they were able to drive through traffic and even ride bicycles. The human brain made adjustments, and each person was no longer aware of seeing upside down. As far as they were concerned, they were seeing right-side up.

Little did they know that when the glasses were removed, the experiment had just begun. One by one, as the participants removed the glasses, they immediately fell over. Their brains had adjusted so well to seeing through the inverted glasses that when the participants removed them, everything they saw seemed to be upside down. It took several weeks for their brains to readjust to not wearing the glasses, but eventually each of the participants was able to see the world right-side up again.

Can you imagine? For weeks you're looking at life through upside-down glasses; then suddenly . . . you're seeing right-side up through upside-down glasses. Pretty cool until they rip off the glasses! Then, with your naked eye, you're seeing the world upside down. Freaky!!

Ripping Off Your Upside-Down Glasses

Do you know the one thing that all really successful people I know have in common? They never stop learning! They are constantly growing and developing by reading personal development books and listening to personal development audio recordings.

Additionally, do you know the one thing that almost every "normal" person has in common? He veges out a lot . . . usually in front of a TV or a gaming system.

Oh boy, here it comes. Kent's about to go all ninja on my TV and gaming habits!

Nope, I'm not. I'm not even going to rip on the amount of time you might waste in front of the television or on gaming. Instead, I'm going to try to rip off the upside-down glasses you might have placed on your melon.

Television (and gaming systems too) is called the "idiot box" for good reason . . . it distorts reality and makes people see life upside down. For instance, the news makes it look like only bad things happen in the world. Reality shows champion selfish and abusive behavior as strategies for getting ahead in relationships. Sitcoms mock dependability and responsibility. If you drink in too much of the TV Kool-Aid, you'll be backstroking in a swimming pool of delusional reality.

My advice, though, is not to throw out your TV set or to stop gaming. I haven't, so why would I ask you too. Instead, my advice is to develop a habit that will help you regularly rip off the TV and gaming upside-down glasses that can get stuck on your dome.

The $10 Gift that Changed My Life

Remember my story? Remember how my SAT scores were so low when I graduated high school that I had to take a semester of Developmental Studies and pass all three classes before I could get accepted into college on probation? Well, the areas I struggled with most were English and reading. I was such a bad reader that even as a young professional if I was asked to read something aloud, I would get so nervous that I'd start to sweat. At my first real job, I would occasionally be required to read in front of an audience. Every time I had to do this, I practiced for days beforehand reading aloud, almost to the point that I memorized the script, so that I wouldn't come across as a complete idiot.

In high school, I learned how to study. So, if I took easy classes and really applied myself, I could make decent grades. This allowed me to put on the façade that I was an above-average student; but secretly, I felt dumb. What's more, I couldn't keep up with the reading demands in even the simplest high school class. I had to purchase the Cliff Notes of every book we were required to read in Literature just to keep my head above water. This meant I finished high school without ever having read a book cover to cover.

Upon graduation, like most graduates, I received a lot of gifts. One friend of my parents gave me a book titled *The Seeds of Greatness* by Denis Waitley. Needless to say, with my background in reading, I wasn't too thrilled. I threw the book on my desk and ignored it for most of the summer. One morning in August, however, while contemplating the discouraging fact that I would be sitting in three Developmental Studies classes soon, I picked up the book and read what this lady had written inside the cover.

> *Kent,*
>
> *If I would receive this as a graduation present, I would probably say, "Oh great, not another book to read." But here it is . . . take your time and absorb this book. I think you are a very special young man with great potential. Seeds of greatness have been planted within you—cultivate them, Kent!*
>
> *—Mrs. Sledd*

The first chapter was titled "The Seeds of Self-Esteem." Because I was such a slow reader, it took me almost two hours to wade through those 16 pages, but I plowed through because it was as if the author were speaking directly to me. The next day I did the same with chapter two. And ten days later I finished the book . . . *the first time ever I had read a book from cover to cover.*

Ripping Off My Upside-Down Glasses

Some awesome things happened to me during those ten days!

For one, I felt a huge sense of accomplishment! It took me around 30 hours to get through a 220-page book, but I did it.

Two, I actually enjoyed it. I read something that didn't just hold my attention; it grabbed me! This was epic for me; so epic that I actually went out and purchased a second book with a similar message and started reading it.

Three, I ripped off my upside-down glasses. Up until that time, my style of learning had been the road of least resistance. I read only what was assigned, and even then I didn't read it, I read the Cliff Notes. What's more, since I had not been reading anything, most of my insights about the world were coming from television. Ideas like the ones I had just read in *The Seeds of Greatness* were not anywhere in the realm of my regular viewing habits. I had been viewing the world through a broken set of lenses and now, for the first time, I saw a way to greatly enhance my eyesight!

Steps to Ripping Off Your Upside-Down Glasses

Here are the steps that will help you rip off your upside-down glasses and start the empowering habit of reading.

Ready?

Don't miss these!

Step One: **READ TODAY.**

There you go; that's it.

Okay, so there's only one step. Sorry if I got your hopes up, but there's really nothing more to it. Just pick up a personal development book and start reading. It's that simple.

But this I promise you . . . if you start this habit and read even just a few pages a day, it will radically change your life! You'll rip off the upside-down eyeglasses through which "normal" people view life and constantly be introduced to new ideas and strategies. You'll grow personally, relationally, professionally, and more, giving yourself a competitive advantage in practically every area of life.

Reading personal development books has been one of the greatest factors for helping me, as well as many of the successful people I know, live smart. I know it can do the same for you!

According to a 2006 Associated Press-Ipsos Poll, one in four adults read no books at all in the previous year. Additionally, according to this same poll, the average number of books adults read in a year is four.

What this means is if you simply read ten pages a day, you would read approximately eighteen 200-page books per year. And that's just if you read ten pages per day.

Imagine the advantage you will have in 5 years, 10 years, 15 years, 20 years . . .

STOP Being "Normal"
Action Steps

Visit amazon.com today and find at least two books you'd like to read in the following categories. While you are at it, why not purchase one today?

Personal Development _____

_____

_____

Business _____

_____

_____

Personal Finances _____

_____

_____

Biography _____

_____

_____

_____

Hobbies You Enjoy _____

_____

_____

CHAPTER 6

Do The Opposite

*If you want to be successful in life, simply watch what
most people would do in a given situation, and then
do the total opposite—nine times out of ten, you'll
receive greater rewards.*

—Earl Nightingale

Success is simple.

Really, it's not that hard.

The secret?

Just do the opposite of what most people do, and you'll be successful!

Okay, I admit, I'm oversimplifying. But sometimes simplification brings clarity.

How Do You Do All That?

Kathy and I are asked, more often than you might expect, "How do you two do it all? You both seem to be constantly growing and learning. You stay in good shape. You seem to have a great marriage, a great family, and successful careers. And you are so calm and relaxed about life. How do you do it?"

First, just know it feels awkward sharing this kind of stuff. Probably sounds like we're bragging, but we're not. While we are flattered by these kinds of remarks, *we know* we are just average people with no royal pedigree or amazingly-wicked talents, and *we know* we don't have it all together.

Second, we share a simple answer. We believe the secret to our success is that we usually do the opposite of what "normal" people do.

For instance, "normal" people hit the snooze button in the morning. They eat greasy food throughout the day. They invest as little as possible of themselves at work. They blame others for their mistakes or problems. They really don't invest time in relationships they say matter most, but instead veg in front of the TV or their gaming system for hours. Then they crawl out of bed the next day and do it all over again.

Instead of taking this "normal" approach, Kathy and I . . .

- Wake up earlier than most.
- Commit to reading 30-60 minutes every day.
- Exercise regularly.
- Try to take 100 percent responsibility for our actions, attitudes, articulation, and associations.
- Invest our best efforts at work.
- Choose to see the glass as half-full instead of half-empty.
- Eat dinner with our family almost every night.
- Proactively invest time in our relationship with one another, as well as the relationships with our kids.

Read the list again. Go ahead, I'll wait . . .

After reading it a second time, did you notice how all the opposite actions we take help us succeed in the roles mentioned above (i.e. personal development, marriage, family, and career)? Did you also notice the actions are actions anyone can take—no royal pedigree or amazingly-wicked talent needed? That's why I don't believe I'm bragging when I share this stuff with you. You don't have to have a stellar IQ or be superhuman to experience real success; you just have to do opposite of what "normal" people do.

As I said, success is pretty simple, huh?

Success is neither magical nor mysterious. Success is the natural consequence of consistently applying the basic fundamentals.

—Jim Rohn

STOP Being "Normal"
Action Steps

Take a chance this week by doing something really different—be courageous enough to do the opposite of what everyone else is doing! Simply ask yourself: "What would 'normal' people do?" Then do the opposite. I guarantee you will make a much better decision.

Journal your experience here:

_____

_____

_____

_____

_____

_____

_____

_____

_____

_____

_____

_____

_____

_____

CHAPTER 7

EVERYONE IS AN ENVIRONMENTALIST

*We generate our own environment. We get exactly
what we deserve. How can we resent a life we've
created ourselves? Who's to blame, who's to credit
but us? Who can change it anytime we wish but us?*

—*Richard Bach*

I once read about an unusual crime. Thieves broke into a store and tripped the alarm, yet slipped out before getting nabbed by the police. Upon arriving at the crime scene, the store owner was pleased to discover that not a single item had been stolen.

The next day, however, a man came to the checkout counter with a suit marked for $5.00. Someone else approached with a plastic bracelet marked $450. A designer dress—$2.75. A pair of flip-flops—$295. It eventually dawned on the staff that the thieves who broke in the night before didn't come to steal anything, they had simply switched the price tags!

Thermometer or Thermostat

One reason "normal" people don't live smart is because they have fallen for the ol' switcheroo. They live like thermometers instead of thermostats.

Both thermometers and thermostats measure heat. But a thermometer is passive. It *reads* the temperature of its environment, but does nothing to reset it. It just sits there.

A thermostat, on the other hand, is active. It also reads the temperature of its environment, but then it *resets* the temperature to create the type of environment it desires. It changes the climate!

People in the bottom 50 percent bracket live like thermometers. They don't believe they have the ability to reset their environment, so they just read what's going on around them and adapt to it.

People in the top 50 percent bracket—those who live smart—are different. They don't just read the environment in their lives, they positively change the climate.

Which are you?

You are a product of your environment. So choose the environment that will best develop you toward your objective. Analyze your life in terms of its environment. Are the things around you helping you toward success—or are they holding you back?

—W. Clement Stone

STOP Being "Normal"
Action Steps

What is one thermostat action you can take this week to positively change the climate in your life?

_____

_____

_____

_____

_____

_____

_____

How will you go about making this environmental change?

_____

_____

_____

_____

_____

_____

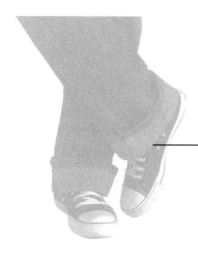

CHAPTER 8

WHATEVER!

Apathy is a sort of living oblivion.

—*Horace Greeley*

During the summers when I was a kid, we played outside all day long. It was baseball in the empty parking lot, exploring the creek behind our house, or soccer in my buddy's backyard. By the end of most 95-degree days in Hotlanta, we were exhausted.

I remember one day, while waiting on a couple of my friends, my legs were so tired that I sat down on a little dirt pile and leaned my head against the side of a building. I felt dead to the world, and as I sat there, I drifted off to sleep.

During my short visit to La-La Land, there was a fogy awareness that ants were crawling all over my legs. Yet, I was so exhausted and sleep felt so good, I actually resisted waking up. I knew that if I emerged from my semiconscious coma, I'd have to acknowledge the ant freeways being built in my pants. I didn't want to deal with reality so for several seconds I convinced myself that sleep was my reality and the ants were just a dream. I finally woke up when an ant on steroids took a chunk out of my left calf. I ran home screaming while beating my legs with a stick.

Taking a Closer Look at *Whatever*

Urbandictionary.com defines *whatever* as "indifference to what a person is saying! Who cares! Get a Life!"

Apathy has long been part of "normal" teenage culture. I went through periods of apathy myself, and I don't think there is one student out of

10,000 who hasn't shown apathy towards at least one thing. So I want to be careful not to diss you if you happen to be apathetic from time to time. The difference between those who live smart and those who don't is the target of their apathy. Let me give you some examples . . .

If you are indifferent about who wins the World Series, or if you say "whatever" to the fact that it's hotter today than it was yesterday, that sort of apathy really doesn't matter in the grand scheme of life. However, if you are apathetic about things like preparing for your future, about the influence of friends, or about following through with your commitments, then your "whatever" attitude is a lot like trying to sleep through an ant attack. You're dreaming if you think it isn't a big deal.

Act As If

If you happen to have an apathy chip sitting on your shoulder right now, I could give you loads of advice about setting goals and making plans; but honestly, when I struggle with apathy, I don't have the energy to set goals or make plans. That's what makes apathy so dangerous—it's an energy zapper! So here are two simple actions you can take to wake up from the nightmare of apathy, even if your energy is almost gone.

First, admit to yourself that you are apathetic about things that do matter. Just being honest with yourself will increase your energy because truth is powerful. You have probably heard the saying: "The truth will set you free." Well, being honest with yourself will give you the energy to free yourself from apathy.

Second, even if you don't care, act as though you do. If you "act as if" you already have a particular character trait that you want in your life, you will create the conditions for that character trait to manifest itself within your life. Sure, you might have to fake it for a while, but soon you'll notice you are engaging more, listening more, learning more, growing more, and now . . . magically . . . you are no longer faking it because you actually care more!

Apathy is the glove into which evil slips its hand.

—Bodie Thoene

STOP Being "Normal"
Action Steps

Are you struggling with apathy? Pick one area that you know you need to care more about and write a few thoughts on how you can "act as if" you care.

_____

_____

_____

_____

_____

_____

_____

_____

_____

_____

_____

_____

_____

_____

_____

_____

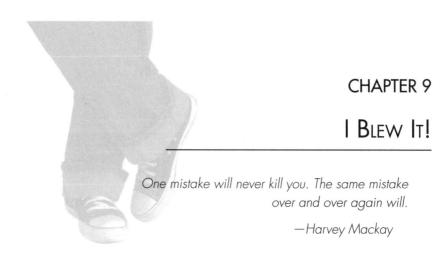

CHAPTER 9

I BLEW IT!

*One mistake will never kill you. The same mistake
over and over again will.*

—Harvey Mackay

Guess what?

You're going to blow it from time to time.

Wow! I'll bet you're thinking, "Thanks, Captain Obvious. Any other astounding insights you want to dazzle me with?"

Actually, yes . . .

Now What?

If you're like me, you don't like screwing up. I'm not talking about trivial blunders like miscalculating an algebra problem or forgetting to pick something up from the store. I'm talking about really blowing it—dropping the ball, intentionally or unintentionally, in some major way. I hate this kind of mistake!

Additionally, if I blow it on a project or assignment, that's not good, but it's not catastrophic either. But when a mess-up involves other people . . . that's the worst. For instance, recently I blew it when making a decision. The decision itself wasn't bad, but I dropped the ball in how I communicated the decision and that negatively impacted someone pretty significantly. Ouch!

As I've attempted to work through this mistake, I've thought quite a bit about what I did wrong, what I could have done differently, and how important the right response is when making a mistake. I'll share what I've learned, and I hope it will equip you to better navigate those times when you blew it.

What I Did Wrong

As I said, the decision I made wasn't wrong, but I really messed up in communicating it. Without sharing too much information, the bottom line is I waited too long to inform the person regarding what was happening. My lack of communication ended up communicating that I didn't respect this individual; something that is not true, but something that was rightfully felt because of my lack of action.

What did I learn? I learned that I can gab on and on about respecting people, but if I don't back up my talk with the right actions, then my words are pretty empty.

What I Could Have Done Differently

What I should have done from day one was step into this person's shoes. If I had, I would have seen how important this issue was to the individual. And let me get gut level honest—it's not as though I needed to be Sherlock Holmes to figure out that this decision was going to significantly impact this person. It was as obvious as gravity. I have no excuse; I simply didn't pay attention. Ahhh, something we've already said is critical for success.

How to Respond When a Mistake is Made

As Captain Obvious has already stated, we all make mistakes. It's part of life. So here are some steps I've learned to take when I blow it. They don't always resolve the problem—no action can guarantee that—but they do cause me to take responsibility for my goof-ups so that my mistakes don't get the best of me.

Run at the problem. Once I realize I've blown it, I run *at* the problem, not away from it. I try to face up to the situation and meet it head-on rather than trying to avoid it. In fact, avoidance, whether intentional or not, is often the reason a problem starts in the first place, so more of the same isn't going to bring about a solution.

Take ownership by asking for forgiveness. I don't just say, "I'm sorry." I ask for forgiveness. There is something powerful in going beyond just *telling* someone I am sorry and instead *humbling myself and asking* the person to do something for me that I don't deserve. Whether a person forgives me or not, asking for forgiveness is my way of really owning my mistake.

Make amends. If there is something I can do to make the situation right, I offer to do that.

Don't get stuck. Sometimes a person refuses to forgive me. If this happens, it's in everyone's best interest over time to continue to try to foster resolution. However, if resolution doesn't come about, there's not much more I can do. And while I dislike unresolved issues, I cannot allow myself to be controlled by another person. Therefore, there comes a time I have to simply say, "There's nothing more I can do," and move on. It's not the best alternative, but it is the best alternative given the situation.

Learn and grow. As I've been saying, successful people continually learn and grow, and they usually grow more from their mistakes than their successes. So while I hate blowing it, I'm not going to waste a mistake by not learning and growing from it.

Mistakes are painful when they happen, but years later a collection of mistakes is what is called experience.

—Denis Waitley

STOP Being "Normal"
Action Steps

Have you blown it recently? Really blown it? Write out how you can take the following steps to ensure that your mistake doesn't get the best of you.

Run at the problem: _____

_____

_____

Take ownership by asking for forgiveness: _____

_____

_____

Make amends: _____

_____

_____

Don't get stuck: _____

_____

_____

Learn and grow: _____

_____

_____

CHAPTER 10

Who Am I?

*We are what we repeatedly do. Excellence, then, is
not an act, but a habit.*

—*Aristotle*

I am your constant companion,
I am your greatest helper or your heaviest burden.
I will push you onward or drag you down to failure.
I am at your command.
Half of the tasks that you do you might just as well
Turn over to me and I will do them quickly and correctly.

I am easily managed,
You must merely be firm with me.
Show me exactly how you want something done;
After a few lessons I will do it automatically.
I am the servant of all great people and
Alas, of all failures as well.
Those who are great I have made great,
Those who are failures I have made failures.

I am not a machine, but I work with all the precision
Of a machine, plus the intelligence of a person.
Now you may run me for profit or
You many run me for ruin.
It makes no difference to me.
Take me, train me, be firm with me,
And I will lay the world at your feet.
Be easy with me and I will destroy you.

Who Am I?
I Am Called HABIT.

—Author Unknown

I started this first section—the *LIVE Smart* section—by saying I'm amazed by how many people live dumb. Not to be a jerk, but there are a lot of people who do outright stupid stuff and wonder why life doesn't work for them.

As we transition to Section Two—the *It's Your Life, Own IT* section—I want to point out something very important. This first section has focused on *habits to survive*. The next section spotlights *habits to thrive*. The final section zeros in on *habits to fly*. Notice a common theme? Real success revolves around *habits*.

But guess what? So does failure.

What this means is that *the habits we develop determine the direction and destiny of our lives.*

Read that last line again . . . S-L-O-W-L-Y. Pretty significant, isn't it? As the maxim states: "Sow a thought, reap an action; sow an action, reap a habit; sow a habit, reap a character; sow a character, reap a destiny."

Before transitioning to the next section, here is a story that should put the power of habits into perspective.

The Tree of Life

There are a bunch of trees in my backyard. A few are saplings. A few are two or three feet tall. Several are six to twelve feet tall. And there are over a dozen enormous trees over a hundred feet tall.

When my son was younger, we were in the backyard together and I pointed towards a little sapling. I asked him if he thought I could pull it out by its roots. He said, "Sure, Dad," and with that I yanked it out. (I know, I'm such a stud.)

Next, I pointed to a tree that was about three feet high. I asked Chris if he thought I could pull this one out of the ground. He thought I could, so I did. I had to really jerk the tree from side to side and work on it for a while, but I finally yanked it out as well.

Now, with sweat dripping from my shiny bald head, I pointed to a tree that was about ten feet high. I asked once again if he thought I could pull this tree out by its roots. This time he shook his head no. I explained that if I got a shovel out and dug around the tree I could probably uproot it, but that it would take me several hours and a ton of work.

I finally pointed to one of the monstrous, 100-foot trees and asked if he thought I could pull this tree out by its roots even with a shovel. He said, "No way!"

That's when I made my point. Our lives are like trees with our habits being the roots. When we're young our habits are not yet established, so they are easy to root out. As we grow older, however, the habits we develop grow deeper and deeper. One day, our habits are going to be so deeply ingrained that they will be as strong as the roots of a 100-foot oak tree. The question for each of us is: Will our habits be roots that grow into success or enslave us to failure?

Excellence is not a singular act, but a habit. You are what you repeatedly do.

—Shaquille O'Neal

First we make our habits, then our habits make us.

—Charles C. Noble

STOP Being "Normal"
Action Steps

What good habits have you established in your life? What can you do to continue to grow these roots deeper?

_____

_____

_____

_____

_____

_____

What bad habits have you developed? What can you do to uproot these habits and replace them with more positive ones?

_____

_____

_____

_____

_____

_____

_____

It's Your Life— Own IT!

What lies behind us and what lies ahead of us are tiny matters to what lies within us.

—Ralph Waldo Emerson

Perhaps the greatest roadblock that keeps people stuck in a "normal" life is excuses. *It's not my fault. I can't. I don't know how. I'm not talented enough. Things never go my way.*

You get the picture!

Do you know the definition of an excuse? An excuse is a lie wrapped in a reason.

If you want to move from the 50 percent bracket to the top 10 percent bracket you'll have to stop lying to yourself, dump your excuses, and start owning your life. Do this and you're guaranteed to live "beyond average."

I call the habits in this section *habits to thrive.*

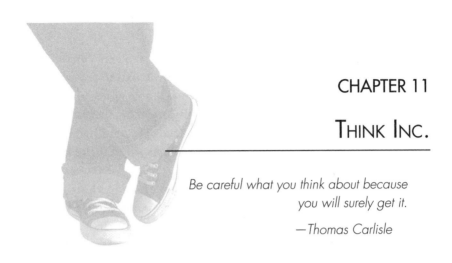

CHAPTER 11

THINK INC.

*Be careful what you think about because
you will surely get it.*

—Thomas Carlisle

If you are serious about moving into the top 10 percent bracket and owning your life, then, starting today, I want you to go into business for yourself. I even have a name for your company: *Think Inc.*

Now, before jumping in with both feet, you need to know a few things
about this business. First off, your role in *Think Inc.* is that of the CEO
(Chief Executive Officer). This means the buck stops with you! You are
100 percent responsible for what your company produces and the results
you deliver. Additionally, it's your job to make sure the company continues
to grow and remains profitable. Finally, both success and failure ride solely
on your shoulders.

By the way, in case you're wondering what product *Think Inc.* manufac-
tures, it's your thoughts!

Still want the job?

You Become What You Think About Most

If you want to experience real success in the most important roles of
your life, then one of the best *thrive* habits you can foster is to intentionally and proactively own your thinking. Intentional and proactive thinking does not mean you have to have an Einstein IQ, it simply means that
you are "on purpose" with your thoughts and that you "initiate plans" to

pursue your purpose. Here are some quick guidelines that should help you own your thinking and launch your *Think Inc.*

Protection. As suggested in Chapter One, life is like a Simon Says game—it's designed to get you out. This means you need to protect yourself from destructive thinking patterns. The black hole of negative thinking exists everywhere! 24-7 news cycles. Pornographic websites. Shallow celebrity culture. If you don't stand guard at the entrance of your mind, you'll get sucked away in no time. It takes intentional effort to protect your mind.

People. One of the best ways to guard against destructive thinking is to hang out with the right kind of people. We'll address this more in Chapter Nineteen, but for now, just know that connecting with friends and mentors who are intentional and proactive in their thinking is a great way to remain intentional and proactive in your thinking.

Purpose. In the next chapter we'll take an in-depth look at how to determine your purpose in life; but again, for now, just know that embracing your life's purpose will cause you to take major ownership of your *Think Inc.* company. As Jim Rohn states, "If you don't design your own life plan, chances are you'll fall into someone else's plan. And guess what they have planned for you? Not much."

Plan. Once you tap into your purpose, you can't take a break from thinking. To accomplish that purpose, you must develop a plan. As Stephen Brannon says, "Opportunities are converted to success by having a definite plan in which you fervently believe and upon which you must vigorously act. There is no other route to success." Well said! And I love what Eleanor Roosevelt said: "It takes just as much time and energy to wish as it does to plan." If this is true, and I think it is, we might as well spend our time and energy creating a solid plan. And guess what? This is a subject we tackle big time in Section Three.

Persistence. Finally, once you have a plan, if you aren't willing to persistently pursue that plan it's as worthless as the two-cent piece of paper it's written on. As W. Clement Stone wrote, "No matter how carefully you plan your goals, they will never be more than pipe dreams unless you pursue them with gusto." This means we must follow the advice that Christian Bovee gives: "The method of the enterprising is to plan with audacity and execute with vigor." We'll tackle the concept of persistence with gusto and vigor in Section Three as well.

To wrap it up, James Allen said, "A person is literally what he thinks, his character being the complete sum of all his or her thoughts." He also believed that "every action and feeling is preceded by a thought." Good reasons to start your *Think Inc.* company today!

Whether you think you can or think you can't, you're right.

—Henry Ford

STOP Being "Normal"
Action Steps

What are you doing or what do you need to do to **protect** your thinking?

_____

_____

Are you allowing **people** to be positive or negative influences on your thinking?

_____

_____

Do you have a personal **purpose** statement that shapes your thinking?

_____

_____

Are you following a well thought-out **plan** to live out your life's purpose?

_____

_____

Are you **persistently** pursuing your well thought-out plan?

_____

_____

_____

CHAPTER 12

ON MISSION?

Find a purpose in life so big it will challenge every capacity to be at your best.

—David O. McKay

One year a television program preceding the Winter Olympics featured blind skiers. Yup, you read that right, blind skiers!

As crazy as it sounds these skiers were trained for slalom skiing. Each one was paired with a sighted skier. At first, the blind skiers were taught how to make right and left turns on bunny slopes. Once turns were mastered, they were taken to slalom slopes. As they skied down the slopes their sighted partners skied right beside them shouting, "Left!" and "Right!" It was totally epic—blind skiers depending 100 percent on the sighted skiers' words. Complete trust!

What a vivid picture of the power of knowing our life's mission! The truth is, we have no idea what is going to happen to us in five years, three years, one year . . . even today. We are like blind skiers flying down a ski slope. Yet a clear mission acts as a sighted skier shouting out directions as we approach each opportunity or obstacle that pops up in our lives.

The Three Biggies!

"Normal" teenagers don't do life mission statement. But remember, who wants to be "normal?" I wrote my first mission statement in my late teens and it instantly catapulted me towards a more focused and intentional life. You can do the same!

Wondering how to go about writing a life mission statement? Easy . . . just answer the three big questions of life:

- What **one thing** is most important in your life?
- How does this one thing impact who you want to **be**?
- How does this one thing influence what you want to **do** with your life?

Okay, I confess. Combining the word "easy" with the phrases "life mission" and "the three big questions of life" creates the ultimate oxymoron. The truth is, scribbling out your life mission statement will likely take hours, weeks, months, even years to get it just right. What's more, over the years you'll tweak your mission as you learn more about yourself, your passions, and life in general.

Yet, if you want to thrive, then the time to start thinking about the three big questions of life is now. You don't have to figure everything out perfectly to start living into your purpose. As General George Patton said, "A good plan implemented today is better than a perfect plan implemented tomorrow." So let's take a stab at answering the three biggies!

What's Your *One Thing*?

My company, Live It Forward LLC, conducts life and career coaching for clients all over the United States, and in the past six years, I've personally coached over 400 people in discovering their life mission. To start the process, I always ask the same question: "If you had to boil all of life down to one thing that makes life significant and meaningful for you, what would that one thing be?" In response, my clients almost always ask this question: "How in the world can I narrow life down to one thing?"

I admit, it's hard, but answering this question is the key to discovering the big picture of our lives. This means we need to cowboy up and answer the question, no matter how tough it might be.

Perhaps a scenario will help. Imagine that from this moment on, everything in life goes as well as it could for you. Not that life is perfect, because that's unrealistic, but envision a life in which your relationships are rich and meaningful, you invest in work you absolutely love, you achieve the goals you set for yourself, and you make meaningful contributions to the world. You live such an amazing life that when you get to the end of it, you look back and say, "I'm the most blessed person to ever live—I wouldn't change a thing!" Get a clear picture of this in your head and heart. Really feel what this would feel like deep within.

Now . . . imagine the exact opposite. Imagine the most horrific life you could imagine. I'm not talking about job troubles or not accomplishing some goal you set out for yourself; I'm talking about experiencing horrendous difficulties, even persecution, that you wouldn't wish on your worse enemy. Get a clear picture of what this would feel like as well.

In order to discover your *one thing*, it has to be something that makes life meaningful and significant in either of these extreme scenarios, as well as in all other realities you could experience in between. You see, we're not in control of most of the events that happen in our lives; we are simply in control of our responses to these events. This means our *one thing* must be big enough that we can achieve it every day in the midst of good or bad circumstances.

For instance, I personally believe that humans were created by God and that He is involved in our daily lives. So my *one thing* statement is "to serve God with my life." A statement like mine might fit your life well, but since everyone has different priorities, allow me to share several other *one thing* statements from actual clients of mine:

- To live honestly and contently.
- To remain positive and hopeful no matter what life brings my way.
- To invest my life well every single day.

Again, the key is to make sure you can live out your *one thing* every day no matter what comes your way.

Go ahead—give it a try. What would you write for your *one thing* statement?

_____

_____

_____

Who Do You Want to *BE*?

Okay, it's time to get all morbid on you again. Do you remember the "attend your own funeral" exercise? Go back to that scene. I know, nasty . . . but bear with me.

Imagine the people closest to you standing up during the ceremony and sharing about your life. What would you want your family and friends say about you as a person? Not what you did, but who you were. What would you want your future spouse and children to say? Think about the character traits you would want them to share. There are dozens of traits to pick from, but narrow it down to the top three or four traits for which you want to be best known.

Once you determine your top three or four character traits, you are ready to craft your *being* statement. Again, here is my *being* statement along with some examples from several clients:

- To live intentionally and proactively in the most important roles of my life (*mine*).
- To be kind, loving, fun, and determined.
- To be kind, generous, and bold.
- To be humble, generous, and joyful.

Okay, it's your turn. Decide the top three or four character traits you want to be known for most, then write them in a simple statement below.

_____

_____

_____

_____

What Do You Want to *DO*?

We're still at your funeral. Another group of people stand up to talk about your life. These are people who you have served throughout your life through work. It doesn't matter if you know yet what you are going to do for work or not, the key is that these people greatly appreciate *how* you served them. They talk about what you did for them, how you did it, and the impact you made on them. Your contribution was obviously valuable and meaningful!

Just as before, you must put these thoughts into a statement. And honestly, this might be the hardest of the three; at least it is for most of my clients. So here are some examples that should help you out:

- To inspire and equip people and organizations to live it forward in the most important roles of their lives (*mine*).
- To bring the best out in others through teaching and equipping them to make informed decisions on their own.
- To achieve my entrepreneurial goals so that I can equip others to do the same.
- To advise and lead people and organizations to persistently find positive solutions to accomplish their goals with excellence.

I know this one is especially challenging, so don't get caught up in trying to make it perfect. Just get something down on paper that connects with you:

_____

_____

_____

_____

Putting It All Together

Once you've answered the three biggies, it's time to organize your thoughts into a personal mission statement. This statement can truly be called a "mission statement" because it describes your mission as your *one thing*, it shares who you will *be* to fulfill that one thing, and it explains what you will *do* to accomplish your one thing.

Below I've taken the four examples we've used throughout this chapter and put them into mission statements for you.

- To serve God with my life by living intentionally and proactively in the most important roles of my life, and by inspiring and equipping people and organizations to live it forward in the most important roles of their lives (*mine*).
- To live honestly and contently by being kind, loving, fun, and determined, and by bringing out the best in others through teaching and equipping them to make informed decisions on their own.
- To remain positive and hopeful no matter what life brings my way by being kind, generous, and bold, and by achieving my entrepreneurial goals so that I can equip others to do the same.
- To invest my life well every single day by being humble, generous, and joyful, and by advising and leading people and organizations to persistently find positive solutions to accomplish their goals with excellence.

Life is never made unbearable by circumstances, but only by lack of meaning and purpose.

—Viktor Frankl

STOP Being "Normal"
Action Steps

Put together your mission statement below.

Your *One Thing* statement: ___TO_____

_____

_____

_____

Your *Being* statement: ___BY_____

_____

_____

_____

_____

Your *Doing* statement: ___AND BY_____

_____

_____

_____

_____

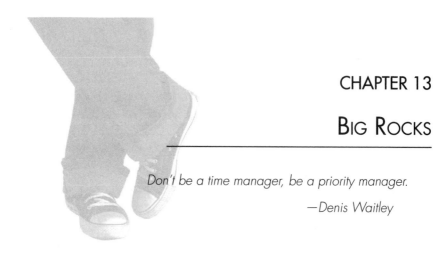

CHAPTER 13

BIG ROCKS

Don't be a time manager, be a priority manager.

—Denis Waitley

One of my favorite authors is Stephen Covey. If you haven't read *Seven Habits of Highly Effective People* (there is a teen version of this book) or *First Things First*, they are must-read books!

In *First Things First*, Covey tells a story that is so visually powerful I've actually created the same experience on several occasions when speaking to youth. Read it for yourself and see what I mean:

> I attended a seminar once where the instructor was lecturing on time. At one point, he said, "Okay, it's time for a quiz." He reached under the table and pulled out a wide-mouth gallon jar. He set it on the table next to a platter with some fist-size rocks on it. "How many of these rocks do you think we can get in the jar?" he asked.
>
> After we made our guess, he said, "Okay, let's find out." He set one rock in the jar . . . then another . . . then another. I don't remember how many he got in, but he got the jar full. Then he asked, "Is this jar full?"
>
> Everybody looked at the rocks and said, "Yes."
>
> Then he said, "Ahhh." He reached under the table and pulled out a bucket of gravel. Then he dumped some gravel in and shook the jar and the gravel went in all the little spaces left by the big rocks. Then he grinned and asked once more, "Is the jar full?"
>
> By this time we were on to him. "Probably not," we said.
>
> "Good!" he replied. And he reached under the table and brought out a bucket of sand. He started dumping the sand in and it went in all the

little spaces left by the rocks and the gravel. Once more he looked at us and said, "Is the jar full?"

"No!" we all roared.

He said, "Good!" and he grabbed a pitcher of water and began to pour it in. He got something like a quart of water in that jar. Then he said, "Well, what's the point?"

Somebody said, "Well, there are gaps, and if you really work at it, you can always fit more into your life.'

"No," he said, "That's not the point. The point is this: if you hadn't put these big rocks in first, would you ever have gotten any of them in?"

(Covey, 1994, pp 88–89)

Your Mission Isn't a Mission if It Sits on the Shelf

The work required to write your mission statement is one of the greatest challenges of this book, so it's extra important that you don't let all that effort go to waste by putting your mission statement up on a dusty shelf somewhere and forgetting about it. That's not what successful people do! Successful people make sure their mission statements act as "self-help" tools, not "shelf-help" gizmos (read this statement again carefully if you didn't catch my little play on words the first time).

Your mission statement is the biggest rock in your life. Plus, it helps you determine what other big rocks you should put in your life. This means the more focused you are on your mission statement the better you will be at putting the big rocks into your daily life first. And hear me on this . . . prioritizing what's most important is a skill you must develop if you want to move beyond "normal." Remember, it's your life—you gotta own IT!

So, in this chapter I have only one suggestion: Every morning when you get up, take three minutes to read your mission statement and think about how you will intentionally make decisions based on your mission. Then, before sacking out at night, reread your mission and evaluate how you did. If practiced regularly, this one action guarantees that you will get the big rocks in first!

Getting in touch with your true self must be your first priority.

—Tom Hopkins

STOP Being "Normal"
Action Steps

Use a worksheet like this to help you live out your mission every day.

Morning Exercise—
Today I will intentionally live out my mission by:

_____

_____

_____

_____

_____

_____

Evening Review—
How did I do at intentionally living out my mission today?

_____

_____

_____

_____

_____

CHAPTER 14

E+**R**=O

*You must take personal responsibility. You cannot
change the circumstances, the seasons, or the wind,
but you can change yourself.*

—Jim Rohn

E+**R**=O.

I was introduced to this equation during a presentation given by Jack Canfield. He explained how his mentor, W. Clement Stone, taught him that this equation, more than any other, explains the results people experience in their lives. Canfield writes about the equation in the first chapter of his book, *The Success Principles* (another book I highly recommend), and states that if you don't apply it correctly, then the other 63 success principles he lays out are worthless.

Events + RESPONSE = Outcome

The E+**R**=O equation states that our *outcomes* in life are not so much based on the *events* that take place in our life, but on our *response* to those events. Let's be sure you grasped what you just read because it's powerful!

If you want to guarantee a "normal" life, than just embrace the E=O myth. In other words, blame *events* for the *outcomes* you experience. Blame weather, the economy, your parents, your friends, your teachers, your coaches, your lack of intelligence, illness, your lack of education, racism, gender bias, the political system, or whatever else comes to mind. But the truth is, lots of people have overcome circumstances like these and many others have triumphed over much greater challenges. These are the people we look up to and admire. They are truly successful; they are heroes! Why? Because they don't buy into the E=O garbage, they embrace E+**R**=O!

By putting the power of E+**R**=O to work for you, you take ownership of your life! Think about it . . . the vast majority of *events* that happen in our lives are out of our control. We don't control the family we are born into, our IQs, what our friends say and do, the economy, or the weather. There is only one thing we control 100 percent—our *responses*! So, if we want different *outcomes*, instead of focusing on what we DO NOT control (i.e. *events)*, we should invest our energy into the one thing we DO control (i.e. *our responses)*.

Life Gets Better When . . .

The day you embrace an E+**R**=O mindset is the day your life will begin to improve. As Canfield writes in *The Success Principles*:

> *The bottom line is that you are the one who is creating your life the way it is. The life you currently live is the result of all of your past thoughts and actions. You are in charge of your current thoughts and your present feelings. You are in charge of what you say and what you do. You are also in charge of what goes into your mind—the books and magazines you read, the movies and television shows you watch, and the people you hang out with. Every action is under your control. To be more successful all you have to do is act in way that produces more of what you want.*
> *That's it. It's that simple!* (Canfield, 2005, p. 16)

In the next chapter, we'll look at a strategy for taking 100 percent ownership of four responses that you completely control. But for now, ask yourself: *Do I embrace the E=O myth or an E+**R**=O mindset?*

> *It's not the external conditions or circumstances that stop you—it is you!*
>
> —Jack Canfield

STOP Being "Normal"
Action Steps

Do you embrace the E=O myth or an E+**R**=O mindset? Take an inventory.

Do I blame other people or circumstances for the lack of results in my life?

_____

_____

_____

_____

What excuses do I make for myself?

_____

_____

_____

_____

What can I change today to start living an E+**R**=O life?

_____

_____

_____

_____

_____

CHAPTER 15

THE FOUR FENCE POSTS OF SUCCESS

*Take time to accept responsibility. Your life is exactly
that—it's your life. It is created by you. You are
constantly making choices, constantly creating new
experiences. And although we can be affected by
circumstances which can seem to be completely out
of our control; essentially, we decide the direction in
which we walk.*

—Nicolas Watkins

I've led more than 100 youth trips, retreats, and conferences, and one thing a leader learns quickly when leading youth events—he or she must clearly communicate the rules.

Interestingly, practically every teenage group I've ever worked with has been incredibly creative. How do I know? If I had ten rules before a trip, I'd come back with fifteen because of the imaginative, but warped geniuses in my group. Before long, I was reviewing a list of "101 Rules Not To Break!"

All this changed once I developed the Four Fence Posts of 100 Percent Responsibility. In a nutshell, instead of focusing on rules, the leaders and I zeroed in on the expectations we had of students. We held everyone 100 percent responsible in the following four areas, which we called "Fence Posts:"

- Attitudes
- Actions and Achievements
- Articulation
- Associations

I explained that as long as students behaved responsibly in these four areas, they were totally free to do whatever they wanted. In fact, the more responsibility they demonstrated, the wider the Fence Posts grew. With that said, the moment they did not behave responsibly in one of these four areas, the Fence Post would shrink because now adult leaders were required to be responsible for them.

Freedom

I always ended my explanation by saying two things. First, notice how many times the root word "responsible" is used in the above paragraph. I pointed out that successful people want to be placed in situations in which they are 100 percent responsible for themselves because they know their greatest freedom is the "ability" to "respond" correctly in any given circumstance (i.e. *response-ability*). Second, I also pointed out that if a person does not have the "ability" to "respond" correctly, then freedom has to be taken away. (By the way, this is why criminals have their freedom taken away.)

We'll look more closely at each Fence Post in the following chapters; but for now, consider these questions:

- Do you want more ownership of your life?
- Do you want authority figures to grant you more freedom?
- Do you deserve it?

One's philosophy is not best expressed in words; it is expressed in the choices one makes. In the long run, we shape our lives and we shape ourselves. The process never ends until we die. And, the choices we make are ultimately our own responsibility.

—Eleanor Roosevelt

STOP Being "Normal"
Action Steps

Allow me to ask you the questions from the end of this chapter again. Do you want more ownership of your life? Do you want authority figures to grant you more freedom? Do you deserve it?

Share your thoughts below.

_____

_____

_____

_____

_____

_____

_____

_____

_____

_____

_____

_____

_____

_____

CHAPTER 16

FENCE POST #1 — ATTITUDE

*Optimism means we **OPT** to view circumstances through positive lenses; believing good things can come even from challenging circumstances. It also means we **OPT** to live our lives accordingly. Both are two of the best **OPT**ions for our lives!*

—Kent Julian

I've heard it said that success starts with attitude. I agree!

Why?

Because, as the saying goes, *attitude is everything*!

One of my favorite books for teenagers is *Success for Teens* by the editors of the SUCCESS Foundation™. Here is what they say about attitude:

> *Your attitude shows itself in everything you do. Your attitude is so powerful that people can sense it before you say a word. Your body language conveys your attitude—you can sense how someone feels by the way he or she walks down the street, enters a room, or sits on a couch. Your attitude determines both your simplest and most complicated actions— from the way you carry yourself to the way you deal with hard times.* (The SUCCESS Foundation™, 2008, p. 19)

Catch the message: your attitude affects your actions, and your actions affect your life. Ergo, the more positive your attitude, the more positive your life! (Sorry, just had to get the word "ergo" in this book somehow!)

Does Positivity Really Matter?

I know it sounds simplistic—*the more positive your attitude, the more positive your life.* But it really is true. Here's a brief example . . .

A few months back, I tweeted and FB-ed the following message: *All product sale $$ at conference I spoke at got jacked (glass 1/2 empty). Just developed better system for product sales (glass 1/2 full).*

Some interesting responses included:

- *How much did you lose?*
- *Found the jerk yet?*
- *Bummer!*

Most people missed the point I was trying to make. I was attempting to say that stuff just happens, and it's our attitude and response to the event, not the event itself, that determines our outcome.

Don't misunderstand; I was NOT a happy camper! I was ticked that someone jacked all the money we earned through product sales. I mean, come on, when I travel to speak, we have to pack up books, ship them ahead of us (or take them with us), set up the display table, man the table, and then pack up all the unsold products and ship (or carry) them back. That's a lot of work!

So at first, it felt like the wind had been knocked out of me. And, to be completely honest, I wanted to knock the wind out of whoever stole our Benjamins. But within a matter of minutes I said this aloud to myself: *What is done is done . . . what can I learn from it?* And at that moment, my perspective changed. My focus was on positive, future solutions, not pouting like a crybaby. I was thinking of improvement, not impoverishment.

The amazing reality is that not only did my perspective change, *so did my attitude*! I can honestly say I was joyful within a matter of minutes. Was I still disappointed that we lost the green? Absolutely! Then why was I joyful? I felt in control. I was taking ownership of what I could own . . . namely my attitude and actions. Plus, I learned a valuable lesson that we implement from there on out whenever we sell products.

YES . . . a positive attitude really does matter! Not dorky positivity that encourages people to put their heads in the sand or chant silly mantras.

But realistic positivity that understands life is life; it includes both ups and downs. What matters most is not the events that happen to us, but our attitude and responses to them!

> The longer I live, the more I realize the impact of attitude on life. Attitude, to me, is more important than facts. It is more important than the past, than education, than money, than circumstances, than failures, than successes, than what other people think or say or do. It is more important than appearance, giftedness, or skill . . . The remarkable thing is that we have a choice every day regarding the attitude we will embrace for that day. We cannot change our past. Nor can we change the fact that people will act in a certain way. We also cannot change the inevitable. The only thing that we can do is play on the one string we have, and that is our attitude. I am convinced that life is 10 percent what happens to me and 90 percent how I react to it. And so it is with you—we are in charge of our attitude.
>
> —Chuck Swindoll

STOP Being "Normal"
Action Steps

The more positive your attitude, the more positive your life.

Do you believe the statement above? Why or why not?

_____

_____

_____

_____

Do you view life through mostly positive lenses or negative lenses? Why?

_____

_____

_____

_____

What can you do to improve your positivity lenses?

_____

_____

_____

_____

CHAPTER 17

FENCE POST #2 — ACTIONS

*What you believe in is evidenced by
how you live, not just by what you say.*

—Ken Davis

In the last chapter, I explained how our attitude affects our actions, and our actions affect our lives. Let's take a look at our actions.

Remember what we talked about in the introduction? That *big is little and little is big*? That if we want the big things in life, we have to be willing to take the little steps day in and day out that lead to the big things? Well, taking 100 percent responsibility for our actions means we realize that every action, no matter how big or small, moves us closer to success or further away from it.

Lemonade and Chocolate Milk

At one conference I led for about 7,000 high school students, a speaker pulled out a bottle of chocolate milk and a bottle of lemonade during the middle of his talk. He proceed to take a gulp of lemonade and said, "Wow, I loooooove lemonade!" Next, he threw back a swig of chocolate milk and said, "But man, do I loooooooove chocolate milk!" He went back and forth several times, and with each swallow, his face turned a deeper shade of green. Finally he said, "Since I love each drink so much, I should just mix them together and guzzle it down." And that's exactly what he did . . . as the entire audience tried not to lose their lunch!

Once everyone finished groaning in disgust, the speaker explained that no one experiences true success by mixing good actions with bad actions.

That mixture just makes us miserable! Of course, his point wasn't that successful people never screw up; it was that some people say they want success, yet consciously take actions they know are wrong. For instance, saying you want to succeed, yet willfully choosing to cheat, gossip, take drugs, steal, lie, and bully others accomplishes exactly what mixing chocolate milk and lemonade accomplishes . . . it just makes you sick!

I Promise

What can you do to make sure your actions are positive? One approach is to develop a philosophy that instinctively causes you to take the right actions in any situation. In fact, why not just follow the *I Promise* philosophy developed by former UCLA basketball coach and winner of ten NCAA Basketball Championships, John Wooden?

1. **Promise** yourself that you will talk health, happiness, and prosperity as often as possible.
2. **Promise** yourself to make all your friends know there is something in them that is special that you value.
3. **Promise** to think only of the best, to work only for the best, and to expect only the best in yourself and others.
4. **Promise** to be just as enthusiastic about the success of others as you are about your own.
5. **Promise** yourself to be so strong that nothing can disturb your peace of mind.
6. **Promise** to forget the mistakes of the past and press on to greater achievements in the future.
7. **Promise** to wear a cheerful appearance at all times and give every person you meet a smile.
8. **Promise** to give so much time to improving yourself that you have no time to criticize others.
9. **Promise** to be too large for worry, too noble for anger, too strong for fear, and too happy to permit trouble to press on you.

Did you notice that all nine promises are positive actions? They are all positive investments we can make in ourselves, as well as the lives of others. That's an amazingly cool philosophy, if you ask me!

The Bullhorn of Our Actions

Another way to make sure that our actions are positive is to remember the quote at the beginning of this chapter by Ken Davis that says: "What you believe in is evidenced by how you live, not just by what you say." Read it again S-L-O-W-L-Y and let it really sink in.

The truth is, we can yap about what we believe until we're blue in the face, but if we don't back it up with the way we live, we really don't believe it. As the saying goes, our actions speak louder than our words!

So, what do your actions say about you?

If we want to direct our lives, we must take control of our consistent actions. It's not what we do once in a while that shapes our lives, but what we do consistently.

—Anthony Robbins

STOP Being "Normal"
Action Steps

Are you taking any actions in your life right now that are leading you away from real success?

_____

_____

_____

_____

What steps can you take to change directions?

_____

_____

_____

_____

What positive actions are you taking in your life?

_____

_____

_____

_____

How can you build on these positive actions?

_____

_____

_____

CHAPTER 18

Fence Post #3 — Articulation

The language we use to communicate with one another is like a knife. In the hands of a careful and skilled surgeon a knife can work to do great good. But in the hands of a careless or ignorant person a knife can cause great harm. Exactly as it is with our words.

—Unknown

"Sticks and stones may break my bones, but words will never hurt me."

Wrong! Soooooooooooo wrong!!

Words = power. Power to influence others, but also power to influence our own lives. The words we choose either build people up or tear them down . . . including ourselves.

Watch Your Thoughts!

Let's start with how your words impact you. In Chapter Three we talked about how to "Chuck Norris" your potty mouth, but if you only go ninja on cusswords in your vocab, you'll only get to "normal." If you want to thrive and move beyond "normal," you'll have to also "Chuck Norris" negative self-talk. Why? Because what you *say* about yourself is what you eventually *see* in yourself.

People blabber to themselves all the time. They might not talk out loud (that would be kind of weird), but they do speak to themselves through their feelings, impressions, and thoughts. And the words they say to and about themselves become their reality. As the saying goes, "As a man thinketh, so is he."

The sad thing is, "normal" people think the following kinds of thoughts:

- This is too hard.
- I can't do that.
- I will just screw up like I always do.
- I am not (fill in the blank) enough.
- What do I know?
- I am just not good at (fill in the blank) .
- This will never work.
- I am too shy.
- I don't have a chance.
- No one will ever notice.

This kind of self-talk is very "normal." But as we keep saying, who want to be "normal?" "Normal" self-talk will have us wallowing in the mud of our own self-pity, and we don't want that.

At the same time, let me remind you that I personally understand why we talk trash to ourselves. Remember my story? I had a challenging speech problem as a young boy and was basically illiterate in third grade. My SAT scores were so low when I graduated high school that I had to take Developmental Studies before being accepted into college on probation. Yet I graduated with honors in both my undergraduate degree and my Masters degree. Is it because I suddenly moved from stupid to smarty-pants? Uhhhhhh . . . nope.

Two things happened. First, I stopped telling myself I was dumb. For years, I had used words like "I can't" and "I'm just not smart enough" to describe my brain. And for years, I lived down to those expectations. Then in middle school and high school I had several teachers who helped me understand that while I faced some learning challenges, my biggest problem was the pile of garbage I was feeding myself. In particular, my senior year literature teacher challenged me in reading and writing. She said straight out, "You have good ideas, and you express yourself really well. Stop focusing on your struggles and start realizing that you are a good communicator who *can* express himself." The more I bought into her words, the less I called myself an idiot.

Second, I replaced negative self-talk with more positive self-talk. Believe me, this didn't happen overnight, especially with my lack of academic abilities. But over time, I stopped saying "I can't" and started saying "I can." What's more, I focused on the few things I did really well instead of the 101 things I felt like I couldn't do, and it was these few things that empowered me to take ownership of my life and move big-time away of "normal" self-talk.

So, just like you "Chuck Norris-ed" your potty mouth, "Chuck Norris" your "I can't" thinking too!

Watch Your Words!

I mentioned how my senior year literature teacher's words changed me. That's what is so amazing about words—they really have the power to change a person. Up until that time, most of what I remember my teachers in English and literature focusing on was what I couldn't do. This was the first time I could remember a teacher focusing on what I could do. She didn't lie and tell me I didn't have challenges, she just pointed out some of my positive abilities and helped me figure out strategies to compensate for my weaknesses.

Taking 100 percent responsibility for our words doesn't mean we only need to own the words we say to ourselves, it also means we need to take ownership of the words that fly from our lips at other people. What's amazing about this is if we focus on just one simple principle about what we say to others, we can take huge steps forward in all of our interactions. Are you wondering what that one principle is? *Always build up; never tear down.* That's it! Do this and you will definitely be abnormal! (Remember, abnormal is a good thing.)

You see, "normal" people tear others down in order to build themselves up. They're so insecure that they only feel good about themselves if they bring others down to their level. As the saying goes, "Hurt people hurt people." Well . . . don't be "normal!" As your self-talk becomes more and more positive, you will discover that you don't need to tear people down to feel good about yourself because you won't be a hurt person anymore.

Catch the message: If you want to stand head and shoulders above the "normal" crowd . . . *always build up, never tear down!*

If someone were to pay you 10 cents for every kind word you ever spoke and collect from you 5 cents for every unkind word, would you be rich or poor?

—Unknown

STOP Being "Normal"
Action Steps

What is some of the negative self-talk you feed yourself?

_____

_____

_____

What can you do to make your self-talk more positive?

_____

_____

_____

What would people say you do most—build others up or tear others down?

_____

_____

_____

What's one thing you can do today to build someone up with your words?

_____

_____

_____

Fence Post #4 — Associations

*What you will become in five years will be
determined by what you read and who you
associate with.*

—Charlie "Tremendous" Jones

Want a snapshot of your life in three to five years? Take the average of the five people you hang out with most and that's your picture.

Friends

I've worked with thousands of students and one thing I know is that no one is unaffected by his or her friends. Friends are like suntan lotion—they rub off on you. So the question is, do you like what's rubbing off on you?

Additionally, most teens who end up hanging out with questionable friends have used this excuse with me: "Kent, I'm just trying to be a good influence." When I taught lifeguard training, one of the first principles I highlighted was that it is easier for a drowning victim to pull a rescuer under the water than it is for the rescuer to pull a drowning victim up out of the water. The same principle applies to "rescuing" your friends. For every one "rescuer" who successfully swims into a group of "victims" and saves someone, I've seen about twenty "drown" via the negative influence of their friends. A better approach to helping others is to build relationships with positive friends, and then invite a struggling person to hang out with your group.

So be honest with yourself. Do you really want your life to look like the average of your three to five closest friends? If not, take 100 percent responsibility for your associations and build relationships with people who are "swimming" in the direction you want to go.

Toxic Personalities

Before moving on to the topic of mentors, let's look at a few toxic personalities you want to avoid. I have worked with a lot of different people—life and career coaching clients, educators, middle school and high school students, parents, business leaders—which means I have had the privilege of connecting with loads of healthy individuals, but I've also had a front row seat to seeing some of the most toxic personalities in action. Here is my list of the seven most toxic personalities I've come across, how to recognize them, and why they are so toxic. (NOTE: Excuse the cheesy labels . . . I was having some fun when I posted them on my blog.)

1. **Manipulative Mary:** These individuals are experts at manipulation tactics. As a matter of fact, you may not even realize you have been manipulated until afterwards. They're great at figuring out your "buttons" and pushing them to get what they want.

   Why they are toxic: They find ways to make you do things you don't necessarily want to do, which means the world ends up being centered exclusively on their needs and priorities.

2. **Narcissistic Nathan:** These clowns also believe that the world revolves around them, but unlike Manipulative Mary, they aren't shy about it. Instead, they overtly demand that their needs be met. They are the ones who make you want to scream: "Life isn't just about YOU!"

   Why they are toxic: Their sole focus is on their needs, leaving everyone else's needs in the dust.

3. **Debbie Downer:** These folks do not appreciate anything positive. If you comment that it's a beautiful day, they remind you

of the gloomy forecast. If you tell them you aced a test, they'll tell you how difficult the final is going to be.

Why they are toxic: They are joy vampires—they suck happiness out of everything.

4. **Judgmental Jim**: If you find something unique and refreshing, they find it "wrong." If you like someone's eclectic taste, they find it "disturbing."

Why they are toxic: Spending too much time with judgmental people can inadvertently convert you into a judgmental person.

5. **Dream-Killing Keith:** Plain and simple, they love explaining . . . in excruciating detail . . . just how silly and impossible your dreams are.

Why they are toxic: These people are stuck in the muck of "what is" instead of "what could be."

6. **Disrespectful Danny:** These jokers say or do things at the most inappropriate times and in the most inappropriate manner. Maybe this is a person you confided in, and he ended up using your secret against you. Maybe it is a friend who can't keep her nose out of your business. Or maybe it is someone who constantly says demeaning things to you.

Why they are toxic: These people have no sense of personal boundaries.

7. **Never Enough Nancy:** You can never give enough to make these individuals happy. They take you for granted, have unrealistic expectations of you, and continually find ways to fault you for things you do while never taking responsibility themselves.

Why they are toxic: They will require enormous amounts of your time and energy, leaving you worn out and used up.

All of these personalities have several things in common. First, the more these people get away with their behavior, the more they will continue.

Second, most do not recognize their behavior as harmful and, as a result, talking to them about it often falls on deaf ears. Third, these habits get more ingrained (and destructive) with age.

Frankly, life is too short to play around with toxicity. My rule is: I gladly help people who truly want to be helped, but I'm cautious about spending too much time with toxic people who aren't making an effort to get detoxified. Remember, it's easier for victims to pull rescuers under than it is for rescuers to pull victims up.

Mentors

Enough talk about whom to avoid, let's talk about whom to seek out. If you want to supercharge your success, seek out positive mentors! This is something "normal" teenagers don't do; but again, who wants to be "normal?" Finding mentors is an excellent way to move away from being "normal" and into the *thrive* quadrant.

A few guidelines will help you connect with the right mentors.

Don't expect mentors to find you, you must go looking for them. Most adults are more than willing to invest in your life if you ask, but they are not going to come looking for you. Sorry, it just doesn't work that way. So you'll have to take the first step, but you don't need to make that step too difficult. Find an adult you respect and start by asking her if she would meet with you just once to give you some advice. Pretty simple!

Do ask mentors to shoot straight with you. Remember my middle school basketball coach and my senior year literature teacher? Both built me up, but that doesn't mean they didn't say tough things to me. A good mentor will shoot straight with you. They'll build you up, but they'll also give you constructive criticism.

Don't expect a mentor to meet with you every week. Successful people have full lives, so if you ask to meet every week with a mentor, he will probably have to say no. Instead, just ask if you can take him out to breakfast or lunch every once in a while and pick his brain.

Do treat mentors special. Notice I said to ask mentors if you can take them to breakfast or lunch. Great mentors could charge you $500 an hour for the advice they dispense, so show them some love by covering their meal. Not only is it a great way to say "thanks," but you will also make an extremely positive statement about the kind of person you are!

Don't miss a meeting. People have set up mentoring meetings with me and then forgot about the meeting. Not only is that a huge waste of my time, it's a clear sign that mentoring is not a priority in their lives.

Do what mentors challenge you to do. Again, I have had people meet with me for a few hours to pick my brain, and I've told them step-by-step what I think they should do. A few months later they want to pick my brain again, but when I asked how it's going with what I already suggested, some tell me that they decided not to follow my advice. When I hear this, I "adios" any future meetings because I have no more advice to give. Respect your mentors enough to follow through with the suggestions they make. Even if their ideas don't work, the next time you meet, you can tell them what happened, and I guarantee they'll give you some new insights and advice.

Mentorship is the premier trait that turns ordinary people into extraordinary people.

—Laymon Hicks

STOP Being "Normal"
Action Steps

What qualities are rubbing off on you from your friends?

_____

_____

_____

Do you need to change your associations? If so, what's the first step you will take?

_____

_____

_____

List a few people who could be potential mentors in your life?

_____

_____

_____

Which mentor will you try to meet with first? What do you want to talk to this person about?

_____

_____

_____

CHAPTER 20

LEAD YOUR LIFE FROM QUIET

It takes as much energy to wish as it does to plan.

— *Eleanor Roosevelt*

I once heard a speaker talk about the importance of "leading your life from quiet" (I wish I could remember who said this . . . whoever it is, just know I'm thankful!). Since then, I have strived to put this principle into practice. I'm not perfect at it, but every year I get better. And every year, I believe I move further away from "normal" and experience more success in each of the important roles of my life. For me, leading my life from quiet revolves around the 6 B's I practice nearly every weekday morning. Before I share the 6 B's, here's a bit of groundwork for you.

Groundwork for the 6 B's

If you want to experience real success, it's important to develop successful routines. While the routine I'm about to describe might not fit your schedule as a student, don't use that as an excuse for not developing routines for your success. Use my ideas as a model, then figure out how to schedule your own success practices.

I begin most days around 5:30 AM. If you gasp at the idea of 5:30 AM, just know I used to as well. By nature, I'm a night owl. I had to learn how to get up early, so believe me, if I can do it, you can too. What's more, your chances of success go way up if you get a jump-start on your day. I have yet to meet someone I would consider truly successful who is not an early riser. I'm sure successful late-morning or early-afternoon risers are out there, I just don't know any of them. Oh yeah, one more thing . . . waking up late is "normal." Enough said!

Most mornings, I invest 40-60 minutes in the 6 B's I'm about to describe, but sometimes I can only invest 20-30 minutes. There have even been seasons in my life when investing 15 minutes is all I could pull off. Whatever situation you find yourself in, the key is to invest whatever time you can! If you invest "nada" minutes into leading your life from quiet, your life probably won't add up to much more than "nada."

Finally, I don't accomplish every "B" every morning, nor do I try to since that's not the point. The point is to invest in a variety of activities each day that "sharpen my saw" (an idea found in *Seven Habits of Highly Effective People*, the book by Stephen Covey that I recommended early). I usually accomplish every "B" listed below at least once a week. The cumulative impact of practicing each "B" every week is:

- Tremendous personal growth and development,
- Better perspective and insight,
- Greater balance in the major roles of my life,
- Real success and thriving.

The 6 B's

1. **Body & Brew:** The first thing I enjoy every morning is a cup of coffee and 5-10 minutes of stretching. It's a great way to wake up and get my blood moving. During certain seasons, I might even get in a workout, but my current schedule is flexible enough that I like to workout during the lunch hour. (On a side note, if morning were the only time I could squeeze in a workout, I'd do it. Exercise is that important!) After I've stretched, I pour myself a second cup of coffee, find my favorite quiet spot in our home, and practice several of the following B's . . .

2. **Blessings Journal:** I've discovered something interesting about myself—I journal inconsistently. When I'm struggling with something huge, I journal a lot! When my struggles are more with day-to-day stuff, I don't journal. I'm not sure why, but I can go months without writing in my journal. That all changed when I started writing in a "Blessings Journal." I basically pick one thing for which I am grateful —a person, place, truth, attribute, value, or something similar—and write one or two thoughts

about the what and why of my gratitude. It takes all of three minutes, but WOW, what a practice! It focuses me on the positives in my life and often leads me to do something later in the day to express my gratitude in a proactive way.

3. **Books:** As you know, I've struggled with reading most of my life, so I don't hold any speed-reading records. Yet every year, I read 30-50 books (yup, I keep track). I have become a much stronger and faster reader simply because I read. Again, I'm no speed-demon, but my speed has probably improved to slightly above average. How do I read so many books every year even though I'm not Speedy Gonzales? By spending part of my "lead my life from quiet" time with my eyes in a book. Think about it—if I give 2.5 hours a week to morning reading (that's just 30 minutes a day, five days a week), then another hour or two a week during the evenings, I can polish off a book every few weeks.

4. **Best Books:** Speaking of books, there are several I read every year. I consider these my "best books" because each helps me stay focused on principles, values, and life strategies that are important to me. *Seven Habits of Highly Effective People* by Stephen Covey is one book I read every year. *The Compound Effect* by Darren Hardy is another. Also, I read a portion of the Bible most mornings—usually focusing on one chapter and looking for a principle I can apply that day.

5. **Big Picture Thinking and Planning:** Once a week, usually on Friday or Monday, I spend most of my "lead my life from quiet" time reading my mission statement and goals. This centers me on my "true north" and helps me navigate how to get to where I want to go. (We'll talk more about goals in Section Three.)

6. **Block Out My Day:** The Pareto principle (also known as the 80-20 rule) states that 20 percent of our efforts produce 80 percent of our results. Because I believe in this principle so strongly, I don't create a To-Do list, I create a *1-20-80 List*™. Basically, after I review my mission and goals, I list all the things I need to accomplish in the upcoming week and place each item in one of two columns. The most important items go in my top 20 percent column and the less important items in my bottom 80 percent column. The reason I call my list a *1-20-80 List*™ is because each day I pick one thing to focus on from my 20 percent column. This way, I am guaranteed not to let the less important activities in my 80 percent column crowd out the more important activities in my 20 percent column.

Bonus Time! There you have it; the 6 B's that help me "lead my life from quiet." If you practice them, it's impossible not to see vast improve-ments in your life. And just because I like you, I'm throwing in an ad-ditional B . . . **BREAKFAST!** Be sure to eat a healthy breakfast with a balance of lean protein, good carbs, and healthy fat. This will give you the fuel you need for consistent energy throughout the day!

You were born to win, but to be a winner, you must plan to win, prepare to win, and expect to win.

—Zig Ziglar

STOP Being "Normal"
Action Steps

When is the best time of the day for you to "lead your life from quiet?"

_____

_____

_____

_____

Which of the 6 B's will you practice during this time?

_____

_____

_____

_____

Any other success routines you want to add that were not mentioned in this chapter?

_____

_____

_____

_____

_____

FORWARD Is The Direction Of Success

Life must be lived forwards.

—Søren Kierkegaard

So far, so good. By "living smart" you move into the 50 percent bracket—the "average" bracket. By "owning your life" you move into the top 10 percent bracket—the "beyond average" bracket.

Now you're ready for the final set of strategies. To move into the top 3 percent—the "way beyond average" bracket—you must push yourself forward because FORWARD is the direction of success!

I call the habits in this section *habits to fly.*

CHAPTER 21

TAKE A STEP!

Every big success starts with a small step.

—Kent Julian

I've been around water all my life. I started working as a lifeguard in high school, then quickly moved up to pool management, teaching lessons, and coaching swim teams. I love swimming so much that when I started my own business a few years ago, I carved out three months every summer to coach a local swim team. It's a huge time commitment on my part, but I love every minute of it!

Over the years, I've easily taught over one thousand little kids how to swim. (You read that correctly . . . one thousand!) I cannot remember most of their names, but there is one little guy I'll never forget. The first day of lessons he marched right up to me, put his mug in my face and announced, "My name is Shawn, I'm four years old, and I hate the wa-wa!"

I soon discovered the extent of Shawn's hatred for the "wa-wa." Teaching little kids how to swim is pretty basic. You start by helping them learn how to "hide your face in the water" and how to "blow bubbles." When I tried to teach Shawn these elementary techniques, his arms and legs wrapped around me like an octopus with nine-inch claws. As he squeezed the life out of me, he shouted at the top of his lungs, "My name is Shawn, I'm four years old, and I HATE THE WA-WA!"

One of my secrets for teaching little kids to swim is if I can get them to trust me I can teach them anything. And one of the fastest ways to get kiddos to trust me is to get them to jump off the diving board to me. Once they do this, their learning curve goes through the roof!

The day I mentioned the diving board to Shawn, he went nuts! He ran to his mom shouting, "My name is Shawn, I'm four years old, I hate the wa-wa, and I REALLY hate the diving board!!" During two weeks of lessons, Shawn never came down to the diving board. What's more, he didn't learn a thing about swimming. He was still Shawn, he was still four years old, and he still definitely hated the wa-wa.

When the next two-week session of lessons came up, Shawn's mom asked me if she could keep Shawn in the beginner's class. I said, "Sure!" That began two months of Shawn showing up for beginner's class every day announcing the same thing: "My name is Shawn, I'm four years old, and I hate the wa-wa."

Then, one day to my total surprise, Shawn came down to the deep end with the rest of the class and actually walked to the end of the diving board. I was shocked! There I was treading water and there was Shawn standing on the diving board looking down at me. I encouraged him: "Come on, Shawn. You can do it! You're Shawn. You're four years old. And you love the wa-wa!"

He just stood there . . . eyes glued . . . not moving a muscle.

After fifteen minutes, I started saying, "Shawn, I'm going to drown. Come on, buddy . . . jump." Finally, Shawn turned around and walked off the diving board. No jumping for Shawn that day.

The next day, he did the same thing. In fact, day after day after day after day Shawn would walk to the end of the diving board and stand there while I encouraged him to jump. And day after day after day after day Shawn would turn around and walk off the diving board. It got so bad that I just started to ignore him. He'd be standing at the end of the diving board looking down at the water, and I'd notice a cute girl sitting up in the lifeguard chair. I'd say something to her like, "This is Shawn, he's four years old, and he hates the wa-wa. I'm Kent, I'm 21, and I love the wa-wa!"

As I was busy flirting, Sean decided to TAKE A STEP off the board. I heard a splash and there was Shawn . . . underwater . . . looking up at me with eyes the size of Hummer hubcaps. I pulled him out of the water half expecting him to grab me by the neck and scream, "My name is Shawn, I'm four years old, and I must terminate you!" Instead, as a wide, tooth-less grim beamed across his face he shouted, "That was GREAT!!!!!"

During the next two weeks of lessons, Shawn learned more about swimming than he had in over two months of lessons. Was his new learning curve brought about because I am such a great swim teacher? Well, of course . . . but that's beside the point. Shawn's swimming skills skyrocketed because he finally TOOK A STEP!

The moral of the story: *Every big success starts with a small step!*

One step in the right direction is worth a hundred years of thinking about it.

—T. Harv Eker

STOP Being "Normal"
Action Steps

Have you ever been afraid to "take a step" in your life, yet when you finally did, you ended up moving forward towards your goal? Journal your thoughts about that experience below.

_____

_____

_____

_____

_____

_____

_____

_____

_____

_____

_____

_____

_____

_____

_____

_____

CHAPTER 22

DISCOVER YOUR PASSIONS

*Given the amount of time we spend working, failure
to find meaningful, significant work is not just a minor
misstep...it is a deeper kind of failure that can make
each day feel like a living death.*

—Dan Miller

If you want to experience real success and live way beyond average, especially in your future career, discovering your passions is a must. In fact, if you can discover what kind of work is so rewarding to you that it feels like you are getting paid to play, you'll never "work" a day in your life. This has been one of the secrets to my success—I go to work every day, but I never feel like I am working!

Don't Get It Backwards

As I've said, my company—Live It Forward LLC—provides life and career coaching services. At the time of this writing, I have coached over 400 individuals to find work they love, so I think what I'm about to say is something I know a bit about.

If I could give only one piece of advice about work, it would be this: *figure out how to earn revenue doing things you enjoy.* You see, I've noticed something about work—people who love what they do have tons more energy than those who are half-hearted or hate their work. In fact, passion for what you do and energy to do it go hand-in-hand, sort of as if they are "twins" of each other.

Interestingly, focusing on one's passion is not what "normal" people do.

"Normal" people focus on money first, passion second. They pursue degrees and look for jobs that promise big paychecks, but rarely stop to think about whether they will enjoy the work.

This approach isn't just bad, it's backwards! I have had tons of clients who chased the dollar signs only to end up absolutely miserable. They have no energy or passion for their work, which means they don't perform well. That lack of performance leads to fewer promotions and sometimes even being fired, which means the Benjamins they were chasing never show up. "Normal" doesn't sound too great, does it?

A better approach is to think about your passion first, money second. This way, you'll have the energy and drive to succeed at work. In fact, Thomas J. Stanley, Ph.D., looked at the characteristics of America's wealthiest people in his book, *The Millionaire Mind*. As he tried to identify what made these individuals successful at work he examined factors like IQ, GPA, college majors, career selection, family opportunities, and more. The only common characteristic he found is they all love the work they do! As I said: passion first, money second.

Finding Your Passions

Discovering your passions isn't always easy, but it can be done. The place to start is to figure out what things might make your passions list and what things definitely don't make the cut. Here are seven questions I ask my clients to help them figure out their passions.

Question 1: If money were a non-issue, what would you do with your life? How would you spend your time?

Question 2: Think about all the times you've said: "I'd really like to do that!" What is your "that?" Write a list of as many as you can.

Questions 3: What do other people compliment you about? What do they say you do well?

Question 4: Think about your big dreams (some people think back to their childhood, but my big dreams were in my teenage years). What do or did you dream about? What thoughts about your future pumped you up?

Now, this advice is going to be different than what most experts say. Don't just think about what those things are and whether or not you could do those particular things—although this is a good first step—think "outside the box" and try to come up with what you could do that would make you feel the same way.

For instance, when I was in middle school, I dreamt about playing college basketball and maybe even making it to the pros. When I realized these dreams were more fantasy than reality (I'm 5'9", slow, and can't jump), I started thinking about how much I would enjoy coaching. So, in my early 20s, I did some coaching in basketball and swimming, but more as a hobby than as a career.

Years later, when I was attempting to figure out how to make the move from work that was okay to something I love, I thought about the reasons I was so passionate about coaching and if I could find something that would make me feel the same way. What I enjoyed most about coaching was inspiring, encouraging, and equipping people to intentionally and proactively make positive progress in their lives. Today, that's exactly what I do through life and career coaching, through speaking to and training teenagers, and through speaking to and training educators. Plus, as I mentioned earlier, I even coach a swim team during the summer. All these passions are rooted back in my middle school and high school basketball days.

Question 5: When you are at a bookstore or the library (great places to be, by the way), in what sections do you spend the most time? What books and magazines do you flip through? When you are surfing the net, what websites interest you?

As a side note, this is probably the best question to ask. In fact, for my clients, this is usually *the* question that helps them tap into their passions.

Question 6: What do you think you do well and what things do you like to do? These things don't necessarily have to be work-related, and they don't have to be big. The key is to name as many things as possible.

Question 7: Let's go back once again to our "attend your own funeral" idea (still morbid, but this works). What do you want your family, friends, and work associates to say about you at your funeral? How do you want to be remembered? For what contributions do you want to be recognized?

NOTE: Portions of these seven questions are adapted from Jean Chatzky's great book, *The Difference* (2009, pp. 81–82). Definitely a book you want to read!

Next Steps

For these questions to work, you must think through them a lot. Take walks and daydream. Think about them in the shower. It will probably take weeks, months, or even a few years to really figure this out. Yet, as the answers begin to bubble to the surface, you'll likely see patterns emerging. Once you unearth your passions, the next steps are to:

- Write them out and journal your thoughts about them.
- Figure out ways you might be able to tap into them at school, at work, through hobbies, or through volunteering.
- Find successful adults who have similar passions and are using them in their work. Interview them to find out how they ended up doing what they are doing, or even shadow them for a day or two to really get an inside look.
- Look for internship opportunities in areas of your passions.

Finally, don't avoid asking yourself these questions just because the process is hard, uncomfortable, or you are afraid you might not figure it all out. If you want to move forward towards work that you are passionate about, you have to have the attitude that no matter how long it takes or how hard it is you are going to figure this out!

As long as we view work as simply something we have to do to pay the bills, we keep ourselves from embracing our talents and gifts, from recognizing our visions, dreams, and passions. Fulfilling work, work that integrates our talents and our passions, work done for a worthy purpose, has always been a sign of inner- and outer-maturity and wisdom.

—Dan Miller

STOP Being "Normal"
Action Steps

Pick one of the seven questions designed to help you discover your passions and write your initial thoughts below.

_____

_____

_____

_____

_____

_____

_____

_____

_____

_____

_____

_____

_____

_____

_____

_____

_____

CHAPTER 23

Play To Your Strengths

A winner is someone who recognizes his God-given talents, works his tail off to develop them into skills, and uses these skills to accomplish his goals.

—Larry Bird

If you want to experience success, don't sweet your weaknesses. This isn't "normal" advice, but we don't want to be "normal," right? "Normal" people think about their weaknesses way too much. Really successful people, on the other hand, *play to their strengths and compensate for their weaknesses.* This is a head-scratcher, I know, so be sure you hear what I am saying and what I am not saying.

I am **NOT** saying that successful people ignore their weaknesses. Not only do they not ignore weaknesses, they are more aware and honest about their weaknesses than most. That does not mean they neglect their strengths to build up their weaknesses. Nope, really successful people understand they cannot be wicked-good at everything, so instead of fighting for perfection, they zoom in on the few things they are really good at and learn to positively leverage those things. AKA, they play to their strengths and compensate for their weaknesses.

I am also **NOT** saying that really successful people make excuses for their weaknesses. They hate excuses! Instead of making excuses, they figure out ways to offset weaknesses. Again, they play to their strengths and compensate for their weaknesses.

A real-life example will illustrate this concept. I am not a detail-oriented person. As a matter of fact, I'm the kind of guy who loses his keys if I do not put them in the same place every night. I use to try to be more detail-conscious, but that got me nowhere. The more details I crammed into my cranium, the more cluttered and clunky I felt. Then I just tried to ignore my weakness and made excuses for myself. This was an even worse approach because I almost lost a job due to excuses. Finally, I started to learn how to compensate for my weakness. I created systems that helped me track important things. My filing system, for instance, plays to the "big picture" way that I think, which allows me to compensate for my lack of details. Also, the way I plan out my week causes me to ask questions about important details that otherwise get overlooked.

Be sure you catch the message here. Don't ignore or make excuses for your weaknesses, but don't go to the other extreme either by trying to be Mr. or Ms. Perfect. Just do what successful people do—play to your strengths and compensate for your weaknesses.

When we're able to put most of our energy into developing our natural talents, extraordinary room for growth exists.

—Tom Rath

STOP Being "Normal"
Action Steps

*Really successful people play to their strengths
and compensate for their weaknesses.*

List one of your strengths and determine a few steps you can take to continue to develop this strength.

_____

_____

_____

_____

_____

List one of your weaknesses and determine a few steps you can take to compensate for this weakness.

_____

_____

_____

_____

_____

CHAPTER 24

PLANNED NEGLECT

*Successful people don't drift to the top. It takes
focused action, personal discipline, and lots of
energy every day to make things happen.*

—Les Hewitt

In his book *Developing the Leader Within You*, John C. Maxwell explains why animal trainers carry a stool when they enter a lion cage:

> *They have their whips, of course, and their pistols are at their sides. But invariably they also carry a stool. William H. Hinson says it is the most important tool of the trainer. (A trainer) holds the stool by the back and thrusts the legs towards the face of the wild animal. Those who know maintain that the animal tries to focus on all four legs at once. In an attempt to focus on all four legs, the animal is over-whelmed by a kind of paralysis, and it becomes tame, weak, and disabled because its attention is fragmented.* (Maxwell, 1993, p. 31)

What a sweet visual as to why focusing on too many things at once will never lead to success. And while there are dozens of strategies I could show you that would help you learn to focus on one thing at a time, here is an approach that is definitely not "normal." In the same book, Maxwell tells another story about a young concert violinist.

> *She was asked the secret to her success. She replied, "Planned neglect." Then she explained, "When I was in music school, there were many things that demanded my time. When I went to my room after*

113

breakfast, I made my bed, straightened the room, dusted the floor, and did whatever else came to my attention. Then I hurried to my violin practice. I found I wasn't progressing as I thought I should, so I reversed things. Until my practice period was completed, I deliberately neglected everything else. That program of planned neglect, I believe, accounts for my success. (Maxwell, 1993, pp. 28-29)

This "planned neglect" strategy is stellar, and it's something I use daily. I determine my number one priority *before* the day starts; then, I work on that priority and neglect everything else until it is accomplished. As a matter of fact, this is the strategy I used to write this book in three weeks!

Want to take a massive step forward towards an important goal in your life? Then reverse the order you usually do things and practice planned neglect!

The shorter way to do many things is to do only one thing at a time.

—Mozart

STOP Being "Normal"
Action Steps

List one major goal in your life right now:

_____

_____

_____

_____

_____

_____

How could you use the "planned neglect" strategy to accomplish this goal?

_____

_____

_____

_____

_____

_____

_____

_____

CHAPTER 25

"NO" Is Not A 4-Letter Word

*Every choice moves us closer to or farther away from
something. Where are your choices taking your life?
What do your behaviors demonstrate that you are
saying yes or no to in life?*

—Eric Allenbaugh

This might sound counterintuitive, but moving forward requires saying "no." Yet saying "no" is a hard skill to develop, especially if you enjoy helping people. Who wants to be considered rude or create conflict because of saying "no?" At the same time, if you say "yes" to everything, you are actually saying "no" to things that are important. Have you ever thought about it that way? I'm not sure about you, but this entire "yes" and "no" discussion makes my brain hurt.

So, let's make it simple. Since forward is the direction of success, successful people learn how to say "yes" to decisions that move them forward and "no" to decisions that cause them to stand still or move backwards. They don't go ballistic saying "no" to every single thing that is not 100 percent mission critical, but they strategically say "no" when saying "yes" is unwise.

Here are a few strategies that will help you say "no" without burning bridges:

Strategy #1—Just say "no." Just say, "I'm sorry. I cannot do that right now." Be authentic and even sympathetic, but be firm. If someone pressures you to explain why, tell them that fitting this new thing into your schedule would cause you to break another commitment you have made to yourself. If the person keeps pressuring you, repeat what you already said, and if they still won't drop it, walk away because now they are being rude.

Strategy #2—Just say "maybe." If you are not sure whether you should say "yes" or "no," you can say, "Let me think about it and get back to you." This gives you a chance to think through your options for a while and keeps you from making a decision too quickly.

Strategy #3—Just say "yes, but . . . " If you want to say "yes," but realize that you cannot agree to everything being asked of you, be honest. Say something like, "I cannot do this, but I can . . . " and suggest what you can do.

Other helpful tips:

- Always be polite, but firm. Show that you are a caring person, but don't fall for pressure tactics.
- If you tell someone that you will think about it and get back with her, then be proactive and get back with her. Don't use this tactic as a way of avoiding a decision.
- As stated above, if someone wants an explanation, you do not have to give a dissertation. The best approach is to be clear that saying "yes" means saying "no" to another commitment. Time is one of our most valuable resources, and since there are only so many hours in the day, we must invest our time wisely.

A "no" uttered from deepest conviction is better and greater than a "yes" merely uttered to please, or what is worse, to avoid trouble.

—Gandhi

STOP Being "Normal"
Action Steps

On a scale of 1 to 10, how well do you do at saying "no" when necessary?

1   2   3   4   5   6   7   8   9   10

Describe a time in the past when you have regretted saying "yes" to a request. What could you have done differently?

_____

_____

_____

_____

What scares you most about saying "no" to people? How can you overcome that fear?

_____

_____

_____

_____

_____

_____

_____

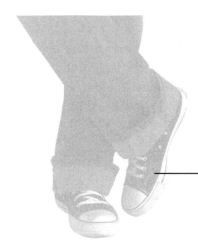

CHAPTER 26

GOAL-SETTING THAT ACTUALLY WORKS

A dream is just a dream. A goal is a dream with a plan and a deadline.

—Harvey Mackey

Goals!

It's shocking how much controversy this word can stir up! When I ask business leaders, young professionals, educators, and even students for an opinion on goals, the responses I get are diverse, to say the least. Here are some:

- Goals kill authenticity and spontaneity.
- Setting goals is essential to success!
- I am in the people business, and you cannot set goals and be relational.
- I have goals; I just don't write them down.
- Setting goals establishes unrealistic, unattainable standards.

No matter where you currently fall on the goal-setting pendulum, if you want to move forward and experience real success, then you need to face reality: *setting goals is not just a nice idea, it is absolutely essential!* In fact, setting goals is one of the most important, if not the most important, disciplines I practice. It impacts every aspect of my life—my career, my personal development, my marriage, my family, my health, my finances, and the list could go on and on.

Got Goals?

I have mentioned goals quite a bit in this book, but we have yet to go into depth about why goals are important, how to set them, and how to achieve them. Let's start with why goals are important.

Goals help you decide what matters most. Nothing creates direction like goals. They cause you to spotlight what you want most in life. Think about it . . . without goals, the issue is not whether you see your targets. Without goals, there are no targets! How can anyone hit, let alone aim at, something that doesn't exist? Goals create targets.

Goals create energy and motivation. Most people wait for motivation before taking action. "I will get in shape when I'm motivated." "I don't feel like finishing this project right now, I'll wait until I have more energy." These equations are backwards! Energy is a result of action, not vice-versa. Setting goals is the forward, proactive movement of deciding who you want to be and what you want to do before motivation exists. Once goals are established, energy builds.

Goals make you smarter. Surprised? It's true! I am not talking about book smarts (although having continuing education goals will help with that); I'm talking about "accomplishment" smarts. People with goals are clear about what tasks are important and they strategize ways to invest their time and energy in those areas. They not only work hard, they work smart.

Getting Goals

Now that you are convinced you need goals—I hope I convinced you—how do you get them? Is there an easy way to write and regularly review goals?

Yes and no.

Yes, there are simple approaches to goal setting; but no, setting and reviewing goals isn't necessarily an easy habit to develop, especially at first. If this answer bugs you, I'm sorry. As you have figured out, I am a straight shooter, so I have to level with you. However, if you are determined to develop the habit of setting and achieving goals, within a short amount of time you will receive huge returns on your investment!

What follows is a brief explanation of a three-step plan I use for setting, reviewing, and implementing goals. I developed this strategy through a lot of trial and error with numerous approaches. On the whole, it's a hodgepodge of ideas I have picked up from various sources and tweaked to fit me. You can and probably should modify my approach to fit your needs. In other words, don't take these ideas as the last word on goal setting, but rather as a model that works well for me and might work for you.

Step One: Group Goals

The first step is the easiest, but most often overlooked. It starts before you ever write your first goal. It is the step of organizing, or grouping, your goals.

People who fail to group goals usually do so because they do not understand the importance of this step. By grouping goals, instead of having 30-40 arbitrary goals listed on a piece of paper, you will end up with a handful of larger objective areas. Each objective area, or target, will have a handful of goals under it. Now instead of aiming at 30-40 random goals, you will have four or five big targets to shoot at. This makes the process of setting, reviewing, and accomplishing your goals more manageable.

As for how to group goals, you can do it in one of two ways: by "areas of life" or by "life roles." The "areas" approach groups goals around areas of life such as:

- Family goals
- Relational goals
- Financial goals
- Physical goals
- Personal goals
- Spiritual goals
- Professional goals

The "life roles" approach, on the other hand, groups goals according to the major roles you play in life. This is the approach I use. For instance, I set goals in the following five roles:

- Personal Development Role
- Family Role
- Career (or Academic) Role
- Social Role
- Stewardship (Serving Others) Role

There are a number of reasons I prefer setting goals around "life roles," none of which I will get into here, but let me just say that the primary reason I use this approach is because I have found it to be a more holistic and integrated approach than the "areas of life" method.

Step Two: Write Out Goals

The second step is the hardest and takes the most time, which is probably why "normal" people do not set goals. It is the process of writing out one-year, three-year, and five-year goals. I do this annually in late November or early December, and it usually takes me 5-10 hours to complete. Although that sounds like an enormous investment of time, it pays strong dividends in three areas.

First, as I've already mentioned, goals cultivate intentionality. This process causes me to think deeply about the goals I want to set and why.

Second, it also pays dividends in time. Having goals frees up five to ten hours a week for me. I do not have hard data to back this statement up, but I know it is valid.

Finally, as I have also indicated, goals help me invest time in what matters most. This means the way I use my time is intentional. How do I know? I track, on a weekly basis, how I spend my time and can quickly see whether what I am doing lines up with what matters most.

Step Three: Develop a Complete System

Even though this might sound cliché-ish, the last step is "where the rubber meets the road" and is what makes my system for setting goals actually work.

For a long time, I set goals, but struggled with follow-through. The reason? Even though I had goals, I rarely remembered to look at them. Once I developed a complete system of implementation and regular review, however, I noticed a huge difference in my intentionality. I am much clearer, on a daily basis, about who I need to be and what I need to be about. Why? Because I regularly review my goals!

When it comes to picking an implementation and reviewing system, there are a multitude of options ranging from the "kindergarten" simple to the "calculus" complex. The particular system you pick is not nearly as important as just picking one. Here are the fundamentals of the method I use. Again, it is a hodgepodge of ideas, but it works well for me.

Yearly goals. As already mentioned, I write out my annual goals in late November or early December. This process takes 5-10 hours. I write my goals for the next year, as well as a few three-year and five-year goals. The long-range goals are more like dreams-in-the-making rather than specific goals. And FYI, as a student, instead of using the one-year, three-year, and five-year approach, it might be better to write out goals for next semester, next school year, and graduation.

Monthly tracking. Once my goals are established, I set aside one day a month to track my progress. I review my accomplishments, change or enhance my goals, and determine which goals I will work on during the next month. Guess when I do this review? That's right, one morning during my "lead your life from quiet" time.

Weekly 1-20-80 List™. I have already mentioned the Pareto Principle, which states that approximately 80 percent of our results are achieved through 20 percent of our activity. Since I have found this to be true in virtually every area of my life, wisdom says I should emphasize the 20 percent activities as much as possible. Therefore, as I stated earlier, every week I create a 1-20-80 List™. I take my most important items—not necessarily the items that feel urgent, but the items that are essential to achieving my goals—and put them under the 20 percent column. Anything else that needs to be accomplished, but is not vital to my goals, gets placed in the 80 percent column. As Stephen Covey says, "The key is not to prioritize what's on your schedule, but to schedule your priorities." This simple approach is a beast in helping me prioritize tasks according to what matters most. It brings incredible clarity!

Daily schedule. When it comes to my daily schedule, the bad news is that time flies. The good news, however, is that I am the captain of my time, which means I can determine the coordinates of where my time flies. So, instead of *time management*, I concentrate on *time investment*. Time management focuses on the efficient use of time; time investment focuses on the effectiveness of time. While I want to be efficient with my time, effectiveness, not efficiency, is the ultimate priority for me. This is why I pick one thing each day (represented by the #1 in the 1-20-80 List™) and implement the "planned neglect" strategy I wrote about earlier. I focus on this one goal first and neglect other things until I have made significant progress on that goal. This simple daily plan guarantees that I not only set goals, but that I also accomplish my goals.

I hope this explanation of the foundational principles behind the goal-setting system I use has encouraged you to set goals that will help you move forward in life. And allow me to leave you with this one key: keep it simple. Do not make your goal-setting system too complicated. Over complicated goal-setting systems = seldom accomplished goals.

An average person with average talents and ambition and average education, can outstrip the most brilliant genius in our society, if that person has clear focused goals.

—Brian Tracy

STOP Being "Normal"
Action Steps

Write out one big goal you would like to accomplish in the next 90 days in each of the following roles.

Personal Development Role: _____

_____

_____

Family Role: _____

_____

_____

Career (or Academic) Role: _____

_____

_____

Social Role: _____

_____

_____

Stewardship (Serving) Role: _____

_____

_____

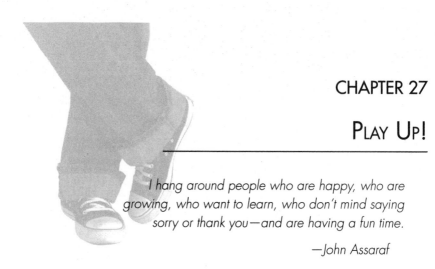

CHAPTER 27

PLAY UP!

I hang around people who are happy, who are growing, who want to learn, who don't mind saying sorry or thank you—and are having a fun time.

—John Assaraf

Since forward is the direction of success, it is important to find ways to push yourself forward. Why? Because success usually does not come to the most talented or gifted, but to those who are willing to grind it out and make little improvements day after day after day after day.

An epic strategy I use to improve day after day after day is to "play up." AKA, I try to surround myself with individuals who are beyond where I am both personally and professionally so I can learn how to "play up" to their level. Any time I have the opportunity to be around this kind of person, I listen and apply what I learn from him or her. This strategy helps me be the best "Kent" I can be.

Some ways I've done this is I've hired personal development coaches. I have purchased truckloads of books and home study courses on topics that interest me. I have also attended dozens of conferences and boot camps. Additionally, whenever I speak at an event and hear another speaker I know I can learn from, I look for an opportunity to treat that speaker to a meal so I can ask questions and gain insights. (Important note: I ALWAYS pay and try to stretch the meal out as long as possible so that I can pick that speaker's brain as much as possible.)

Have these strategies paid off? ABSOLUTELY!

I could give tons of examples, but one happened just this past week when I spent over an hour with a guy who speaks in the education market.

126

He is light years ahead of me both in experience and success, and I mentioned to him that I want to push myself to experience a similar level of success. He stated that it is definitely doable, and as he told me his story, I could hear my story in his journey. I listened, took tons of notes, and am already applying one of the lessons I learned from this man. If you can't tell, I'm stoked!

I could share more examples of how I "play up," but let's instead run through a few ideas that I have seen work well for students.

- We already talked about **mentors**. Definitely seek them out and learn all you can when you're with them.
- Join **student groups and associates** through your school or in your community. DECA (Distributive Education Clubs of America), FBLA (Future Business Leaders of America), FCCLA (Family Career and Community Leaders of America), and Student Council are just a few of the great organizations that are probably on your campus.
- **Visit local business and community associations** like the Chamber of Commerce, BNI (Business Network International), Kiwanis, and Toastmasters (if you want to be a speaker). These groups are filled with business leaders, which means they provide excellent "play up" opportunities.
- Turn your library card into your personal "play up" card. Check out **personal development books and audio programs,** as well as **biographies about successful people.**
- The one magazine you should subscribe to immediately is *SUCCESS* magazine. It's my absolute favorite "play up" resource!

> *Most people have a tendency to settle early in life. They stop experimenting, developing, growing, pushing, and challenging themselves. We have to begin to understand that we must expand or we are expendable.*
>
> —Les Brown

STOP Being "Normal"
Action Steps

What are you currently doing to push yourself to improve?

_____

_____

_____

_____

What group(s) will you join in order to "play up" to a new level?

_____

_____

_____

_____

Have you ordered your subscription to *SUCCESS* magazine yet?

_____

_____

_____

_____

_____

CHAPTER 28

FAIL FORWARD

Failure should be our teacher, not our undertaker.
Failure is delay, not defeat. It is a temporary detour,
not a dead-end street.

—William A. Ward

I'll say it again: Life is like a Simon Says game; it is designed to get you out.

The difference between being "normal" and real success, however, is that successful people understand that failing is part of life. Even more, they use their failures to move forward. Or, another way to say it is: they live their lives with their backs to the past. They refuse to camp out in their history or walk backwards through life keeping their eyes glued to what has been. Instead, they reflect on events in their past, both good and bad, learn and grow from them, and then get their rear in gear and move forward.

To make sure you don't become a victim of your failures, here are a few thoughts that will push you through failure so you can bounce back afterwards smarter and stronger.

It's okay to feel upset. Go ahead, get ticked at yourself; just don't get stuck there. Give yourself a specified period of time to be disappointed. After that, push on.

"Failing" and "being a failure" are not the same thing. In his book *Failing Forward*, John C. Maxwell says, "Every successful person is someone who failed, yet never regarded himself as a failure . . . I think it's safe to say that all great achievers are given multiple reasons to believe they are failures. But in spite of that, they persevere. In the face of adversity, rejection, and failing, they continue believing in themselves and refuse to consider themselves failures" (Maxwell, 2000, 26). It is "normal" to associate failing with being a failure. But we're not going for "normal," so we recognize that failing at something does not make us failures.

Learn, learn, learn. A young businessman was eager to learn from an older businessman, so he went to him and asked, "Can you tell me what it takes to become wise?" The older man said, "Two words . . . good decisions." The younger man said, "Well, can you tell me how you learned to make good decisions?" The older man said, "One word . . . experience." The younger man said, "One last question. How did you gain experience?" The older man said, "Two words . . . bad decisions."

The way you turn your lemons into lemonade is to learn from bad experiences. So don't just get *through* failure, learn *from* failure. You might even discover that some of your greatest failures will end up leading to your greatest life lessons.

Look for new opportunities. Failure can create unexpected opportunities and make the rest of your life the best of your life. For instance, after my first season of college basketball, I realized I was going to be riding the bench for the rest of my career, so I decide it was time to move on. I was pretty disappointed, and this disappointment led to a lot of pent up energy. That led to me running in the afternoons which, to my surprise, I found out I was good at. Long story short, I became a much better runner than I ever was as a basketball player. I won trophies in several road races and still love running to this day. If I had not "failed" in basketball, I might have never discovered my love for running.

On a more serious note, my biggest career mistake led to me becoming a national director of a large youth organization and later, led to me owning my own business. The move that I thought would ruin my career ended up opening opportunities to expand my career. Go figure!

Take a fresh look at your mission and goals. When you experience failure, it is a good time to review your mission and goals to make sure you are moving in the right direction. You might even need to update a few things.

Bottom line, it is a given that you will experience failure. Everyone does! The difference between settling for "normal" and experiencing real success is in how you deal with failure. Remember, it is not so much about what happens to you but about how you respond to it. E+**R**=O!

You always pass failure on the way to success.

—Mickey Rooney

STOP Being "Normal"
Action Steps

Describe a time when you failed at something.

_____

_____

_____

How did you feel?

_____

_____

_____

What did you learn from this failure?

_____

_____

_____

How have you applied what you learned to your life?

_____

_____

_____

CHAPTER 29

ULTIMATE COOLNESS

It's cool to care!

—Todd Whitaker

In high school, I was watching a television show and the guest was a body builder. This dude was huge! He was so big that his earlobes had muscles!! The interviewer asked him, "Why do you develop those particular muscles?" With that, the muscleman stood up, stepped forward, and proceeded to strike several poses that caused his biceps to bulged like a bullfrog's neck. The crowd applauded widely as the muscleman sat down.

But the interviewer was not satisfied. He asked again, "What do you use all those muscles for?" Again, this specimen stood up, turned around, and flexed so that his lats expanded like eagle wings. More applause.

Once more, the interviewer, risking his life, asked, "But what do you use those muscles for?" The body builder was dumbfounded. He didn't have an answer other than to flex his physique.

What a clear picture of how a lot of "normal" people use their gifts and talents. Let me explain . . .

Don't Just Flex

The subtitle of this book is "A Teen's Guide to Real Success and Ultimate Coolness." I've written a ton about real success, but have yet to mention ultimate coolness, so let's change that right now. Ultimate coolness is not "normal" coolness. "Normal" coolness is about popularity and position. It's about wearing the right clothes, saying the right things, and hangin' with the right people. "Normal" coolness is basically selfish because it's all about people flexing their muscles.

Ultimate coolness is different. It's bigger than just our muscles. It's about investing our muscles in what really matters in life. It's about adding value to the lives of others. It's about making a positive difference in the world!

Seven Characteristics of Difference-Makers

Here are seven characteristics of people who have achieved ultimate coolness by being difference-makers. See how many are true for you.

Hard (and Smart) Servers. There is no such thing as easy impact. Making a positive difference takes a lot of hard (and smart) work. If you're not willing to roll up your sleeves and dig in to serve others, the likelihood of your impacting anyone is slim.

Consistency and Perseverance. Making a difference doesn't mean hard work for the short-term as in a service project; it takes hard work for the long haul. How many life-changing stories go untold simply because someone gives up? I would go so far as to say that the people who make the biggest difference are usually not the most talented or smartest people. They are the people who are simply willing to outlast everyone else in the way they serve. That's why great teachers, youth workers, coaches, and leaders can tell story after story of how they have seen peoples' lives change for the better. They have been around for a while, and their stick-to-it approach has been the catalyst that brought about positive change.

People-Person. This is not to say introverted or shy people cannot make a difference in others lives—THEY CAN! In fact, some of the most dynamic difference-makers I've met are much more shy than I am. But while our styles may differ, we are passionate about the same thing—seeing a positive change occur in the lives of others. Simply put, how can you make a difference in someone's life if you are not interested in that someone?

Truth-Teller. Everyone struggles with saying the hard things to others, but difference-makers are willing to say tough stuff because the truth, spoken clearly and compassionately, leads to positive change and growth. With that said, difference-makers know how to balance "directness" with "gentleness." Additionally, they are good at reading people. They know that the same boiling water will harden eggs and soften carrots, so they are careful with how they communicate hard things to others.

Problem-Solver. As we've said throughout this book, problems are a fact of life. Instead of complaining about problems, difference-makers seek solutions. Problems create opportunity for learning, growth, and development.

Lifelong Learner. Difference-makers are always adding extra crayons to their crayon box. Why? Because they know when they think they are ripe, they rot . . . but as long as they stay humble and green, they continue to grow.

Giving. I saved the best trait for last, although you could argue that this is similar to being a "Hard (and Smart) Server." Every truly successful person I know is a giver! In their amazing book, *The Go-Giver*, Bob Burg and John David Mann share five laws about giving that lead to stratospheric success:

- *The Law of Value*—Your true worth is determined by how much more you give in value than you take in payments.
- *The Law of Compensation*—Your income is determined by how many people you serve and how well you serve them.
- *The Law of Influence*—Your influence is determined by how abundantly you place other people's interests first.
- *The Law of Authenticity*—The most valued gift you have to offer is yourself.
- *The Law of Receptivity*—The key to effective giving is to stay open to receiving.

(Burg and Mann, 2007, p. 129)

My advice to you is to start practicing these laws today. Even more, make giving an aspect of every part of your life. In high school I started giving ten percent of my income away to charity and volunteering time to at least one community-oriented organization. These are habits I continue to practice today that add value to my life and help me make a difference in the lives of others. I highly recommend you start doing the same thing!

There you have it . . . seven traits for making a difference. By no means is it an exhaustive list, but it is a great place to start.

You and I want our lives to matter. We want our lives to make a real difference—to be of genuine consequence in the world. We know that there is no satisfaction in merely going through the motions, even if those motions make us successful, or even if we have arranged to make those motions pleasant. We want to know we have made some impact on the world. In fact, you and I want to contribute to the quality of life. We want to make the world work.

—Werner Erhard

STOP Being "Normal"
Action Steps

Journal your thoughts on being a difference-maker:

_____

_____

_____

_____

_____

_____

_____

_____

_____

_____

_____

_____

_____

_____

_____

_____

_____

_____

CHAPTER 30

Stop Sharpening Your Pencil

*Unless you try to do something beyond what you
have already mastered, you will never grow.*

—Ralph Waldo Emerson

A few months ago I recorded a pretty sweet video for my blog. I told the story of how, when my kids were little, they loved using the electric pencil sharpener to sharpen their pencils. In the video, I even gave a little demo. I explain that my kids always wanted the point of their pencil to be just perfect, so they would push their pencil into the sharpener for about ten seconds . . . take it out and examine it . . . push it back into the sharpener for another ten seconds . . . take it out and examine it again . . . jam it back in the sharpener . . . you get the point (pardon the pun). That pencil sharpener would buzz and buzz and buzz as Chris, McKenzie, and Kelsey tried to get their pencils just right. As the buzz drone on and on and on, and just before I went berserk, I would shout, "Stop Sharpening Your Pencil!" Then I'd try to explain to my precious little preschoolers that the tip of the pencil didn't need to be perfect in order to write.

Don't Wait for Perfection

As we wrap up Section Three, let me challenge you to stop sharpening your pencil. Seriously, you do not have to wait until everything is perfect before you move forward towards success. In fact, the act of moving forward often brings about success. This means you don't want to get stuck ruminating too long on what to do, but instead you want to get busy and do something. There's a time for thinking and planning, but there also comes a time when you have to say, "Good enough is good enough" and get off your rear and start moving.

Why not make that time today? Stop sharpening your pencil and make the rest of your life the best of your life. Get moving in the direction of your success!

Better to do something imperfectly than to do nothing flawlessly
—Robert Schuller

STOP Being "Normal"
Action Steps

What are some ways you tend to "sharpen your pencil" and try to make everything perfect before moving forward towards a goal?

_____

_____

_____

_____

_____

_____

What is one positive step forward you could take today to move in the direction of real success?

_____

_____

_____

_____

_____

_____

WHEN ALL IS SAID, BUT NOT DONE . . .

UNDISCOVERED JEWEL

*Success is never an accident. It typically starts as
imagination, becomes a dream, stimulates
a goal, grows into a plan of action—which then
inevitably meets with opportunity.
Don't get stuck along the way!*

—Dan Miller

I read a human-interest story from the 1980s about an x-ray technician named Steve Meyers. He lived in North Carolina, and he had a hobby of collecting rocks.

Personally, I don't get rock collecting. First off, what's the point of wandering around looking for rocks? Second, what do you do with the rocks once you find them? Do you just stick them in a pile in your garage? Or maybe you have a special shelf in your living room where you place them for display. Sorry, but I'm scratching my head on this one.

Anyway, Steve Meyers liked to go out on the weekends and collect rocks in the Appalachian Mountains. One weekend he found a rock that was so cool, he decided not to take it home to the pile in his garage or the shelf in his living room (or wherever else he puts his rocks). Instead, he took it to his office to use as a paperweight. In case you are wondering, a paperweight is a heavy object (duh, like a rock) that people place on top of a stack of papers so that the papers don't blow all over the place when windows are open or a fan is on. So Steve Meyers used this cool rock as a paperweight.

Great story, huh?

Well, a few months later a guy popped into his office and went nuts when he saw the rock. "What is that?!" he shouted. Steve Meyers said, "Ummmm . . . a rock?" The man said, "That's no rock, that's a sapphire!" This guy was an expert gem cutter, and as he examined the sapphire more closely, he said, "Buddy, you better get a safety deposit box because by the mere size of this sapphire, it's worth $250,000." After studying it more closely, he was convinced that it could be cut in such a way that it would sell for more than the Star of America, which was a sapphire that sold in the late 80s for $4.2 million dollars!

Steve Meyers was using $4.2 million dollars as a PAPERWEIGHT!!!!

The Valuable You

You, too, are a valuable jewel!

Yet the sad reality is "normal" teenagers live as paperweights. They might look all sapphire-y on the outside, but their lives don't amount to much more than sitting on top of a worthless stack of papers. That's why I don't want you to settle for "normal." It is too big of a price to pay!

My hope is that you'll strive for the top 3 percent!

- LIVE smart.
- It's your life, own IT!
- And always remember, FORWARD is the direction of success.

Your life IS a valuable jewel. Don't waste it living like a paperweight. Make the rest of your life the best of your life. **LIVE IT FORWARD!**

KENT JULIAN
LAUGH. LEARN. LIVE. LEAD.

Kent Julian is founder and president of Live It Forward LLC (www.liveitforward.com), a personal and executive coaching company that helps people "make the move" to the life and work they love.

Kent also speaks to thousands of educators and teenagers across America each year. When speaking at middle schools, high schools, and student conferences, he focuses on helping teens answer two of their biggest questions: *What should I do with my life?* and *How can I live and lead successfully?* When speaking at educational conferences and in-services, his primary goal is to remind educators what makes great teachers great!

Kent calls this stuff the "blah-blah" stuff. In other words, it's the promo stuff that sort of has to be said in a bio. What he really wants you to know is that he is crazy-in-love with his wife, Kathy, and their three incredible children. One of his favorite pastimes is coaching the Stingrays, a swim team with over 160 swimmers. And just in case you want to treat him to a meal or beverage, he enjoys eating sushi and sipping dark roasted coffee.

You can track Kent down on various social networking sites such as:

Facebook — www.facebook.com/kentjulian
Twitter — www.twitter.com/KentJulian
YouTube — www.youtube.com/kentjulian

For more information or to schedule Kent to speak at your next event, visit www.kentjulian.com or email booking@kentjulian.com.

NOTES

NOTES

NOTES

NOTES

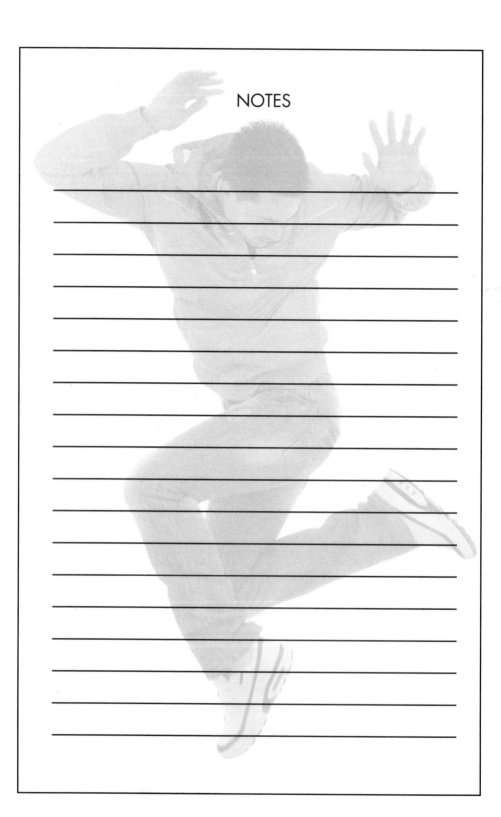